Frank J. Fabozzi, CFA
Professor of Finance
EDHEC Business School

Sergio M. Focardi
Visiting Professor of Finance
Stony Brook University

Caroline Jonas
Managing Partner
Intertek Group

Investment Management: A Science to Teach or an Art to Learn?

CFA Institute
Research
Foundation

Statement of Purpose

The CFA Institute Research Foundation is a not-for-profit organization established to promote the development and dissemination of relevant research for investment practitioners worldwide.

ISBN 978-1-934667-73-6

16 May 2014

Editorial Staff

Elizabeth Collins
Book Editor

Pat Light
Assistant Editor

Cindy Maisannes
Manager, Publications Production

Randy Carila
Publishing Technology Specialist

Biographies

Frank J. Fabozzi, CFA, is a professor of finance at EDHEC Business School, France, and a member of the EDHEC Risk Institute. Prior to joining EDHEC, he held various professorial positions in finance at Yale and the Massachusetts Institute of Technology. Professor Fabozzi also served as James Wei Visiting Professor in Entrepreneurship at Princeton University, where he is also currently a research fellow in the Department of Operations Research and Financial Engineering. A trustee for the BlackRock family of closed-end funds and the equity-liquidity complexes, Fabozzi has authored and edited many books on asset management. He is the recipient of the C. Stewart Sheppard Award from CFA Institute. Fabozzi received his bachelor's and master's degrees in economics and statistics from the City College of New York and his PhD in economics from the City University of New York.

Sergio M. Focardi is a visiting professor of finance at Stony Brook University, New York, and a founding partner of the Intertek Group. He serves on the editorial board of the *Journal of Portfolio Management* and has co-authored numerous articles and books, including the CFA Institute Research Foundation books *Investment Management after the Global Financial Crisis, Challenges in Quantitative Equity Management,* and *Trends in Quantitative Finance* and the award-winning books *Financial Modeling of the Equity Market: From CAPM to Cointegration* and *The Mathematics of Financial Modeling and Investment Management.* Focardi also co-authored *Financial Econometrics: From Basics to Advanced Modeling Techniques* and *Robust Portfolio Optimization and Management.* He received his degree in electronic engineering from the University of Genoa and his PhD in finance from the University of Karlsruhe.

Caroline Jonas is a managing partner of the Intertek Group in Paris, where she is responsible for research projects. Jonas is a co-author of numerous reports and books on finance and technology, including the CFA Institute Research Foundation books *Investment Management after the Global Financial Crisis* and *Challenges in Quantitative Equity Management.* Jonas received her bachelor's degree from the University of Illinois at Urbana-Champaign.

Acknowledgments

We wish to thank all those who contributed to this book, including the human resources managers at asset management firms to whom we promised anonymity. A very special thank-you goes to contributors from academia and the industry who accepted the challenge to articulate their views, based on their experiences in and observations of recent financial crises, on what might need to change in the education of future investment professionals—and indeed in the practice itself. Their views are cited and attributed throughout the book. See the section Opinion Contributors for a full list of those whose views contributed to this book.

We sincerely hope that this book will contribute to the ongoing debate about what we should teach future investment professionals and, by extension, have an impact on how practitioners manage other people's money.

We are also grateful to the CFA Institute Research Foundation for funding this project and to its director of research, Laurence B. Siegel, for his encouragement, assistance, and insightful comments.

Contents

CE Qualified Activity CFA Institute   This publication qualifies for 5 CE credits, inclusive of 5 SER credits, under the guidelines of the CFA Institute Continuing Education Program.

Foreword

Because Frank Fabozzi, Sergio Focardi, and Caroline Jonas have, in this book, looked at the question of how to teach finance from the viewpoint of instructors, I will briefly consider the perspective of a student. What do I need to know? What are the timeless truths I need to understand even if there is no immediate application for them? What are the controversial propositions, and how close are we to resolving them? What is simply wrong?

The basics of investment finance can be distilled down to about eight ideas:

- time value of money,

- discounted cash flow (as the fair value of an asset),

- bond math and duration,

- the no-arbitrage condition,

- market efficiency,

- portfolio efficiency and optimization,

- the capital asset pricing model (CAPM) and market model (alpha and beta), and

- option pricing and optionality.

To these basics, I would add the Modigliani and Miller indifference principles for capital structure and for dividend policy; although these principles are usually taught in corporate finance rather than investment courses, they are very important for making investment decisions. That's it. I'm done. That's the finance course that I'd like to take—I think.[i]

The first few ideas listed are relatively uncontroversial. But when I, as a student, get to the middle of the list, I'm tempted to howl, "Wait a minute!" Market efficiency? The market, says the great investor Jeremy Grantham, is "deliciously inefficient." His vast fortune is testimony to the fact that *somebody* can beat the market. Graham and Dodd and Warren Buffett and practically every hedge fund manager would agree.

So, should finance professors teach market efficiency as a timeless truth, a controversial proposition, or an idea that has been tested and found to be wrong? I would say they should teach it as a vitally important null hypothesis and point of departure for evaluating the claims of those who say they can beat the market.

---

[i]That is the whole course *if* we are dealing with only one currency. The fact of multiple currencies makes finance more complicated, but international issues belong in the second semester.

Portfolio efficiency says that investors should try to build portfolios that maximize utility, which consists of expected return minus some measure of risk. But where are investors supposed to get their return expectations from? What is risk? Is it volatility? Downside risk? Permanent loss of capital? When I go to work in an investment management firm, will I really be building portfolios that maximize return subject to a penalty for risk, or will I be doing something else to deliver the desired results to customers?

The CAPM is another problem area. The CAPM is a magnificent piece of reasoning, but the linear relationship that it posits between beta risk and expected return does not hold exactly. Active management is basically a search for assets with high returns and low risk, which the CAPM says cannot exist. The debate about the CAPM is closely related to the debate about market efficiency. Should professors present the CAPM as a hypothesis, as a well-reasoned framework for thinking about the relation between risk and return, or as truth?

Fabozzi, Focardi, and Jonas, with whom our readers are probably already familiar from their many fine survey-based books for the CFA Institute Research Foundation, address these questions and other related issues in the current work, engagingly titled *Investment Management: A Science to Teach or an Art to Learn?* After interviewing finance professors, employers, and other opinion leaders in Europe, the United States, and Asia, the authors make recommendations for the teaching of finance—investment management, in particular—primarily at the MBA level. They frame their investigation in the context of the global financial crisis of 2007–2009, which caused many observers to question the basics they had been taught in finance courses.

Because of CFA Institute's origins in security analyst societies, the authors have focused on the educational needs faced by such analysts. The decision of what to teach in investment courses, however, affects the broader population now served by CFA Institute, including asset allocators, manager allocators, wealth managers, and marketing and client service professionals. Participants in all of these activities will find this book to be of great interest.

The CFA Institute Research Foundation is especially pleased to present this investigation. A half century after the core of modern finance theory was developed, questioning the basic tenets of that body of work is sensible. Most of the ideas have stood the test of time, but some require revision in the light of experience. Students in our field deserve to know the best thinking of their teachers on these questions.

Laurence B. Siegel
Gary P. Brinson Director of Research
CFA Institute Research Foundation
April 2014

1. Finance Theory: Do We Have a Science to Teach?

In the aftermath of the 2007–09 financial crisis, mainstream finance theory was criticized for having failed to either forecast or help prevent the market crash, which resulted in large losses for investors. Although as of the writing of this book at the end of 2013, markets have recovered beyond precrisis levels, the investors enjoying the recovery are not always the same investors as those who suffered the losses. So, the crash caused permanent impairment of wealth in many cases.

One of the most interesting aspects of this particular crash is that *finance theory*, not simply the practices of the financial services industry, has been directly blamed for the crisis. That is, some observers suggest that the crash itself was the result of bad or poorly applied theory.

Our goal in researching and writing this book was to explore the implications of these criticisms for the curricula of finance programs at business schools and universities and, by extension, for practitioners. We begin with a discussion of finance theory as it is taught today at most institutions. In doing so, we discuss the critique and the defense of prevailing theories by integrating a review of the literature and conversations with academics, asset managers, and other market players.

Although our focus here is finance theory, we also address economic theory to some extent because classical finance theory and classical economic theory share the same principles. Indeed, since the contribution of Eugene Fama (1965, 1970), professor of finance at the University of Chicago Booth School of Business and a corecipient of the 2013 Sveriges Riksbank Prize in Economic Sciences in Memory of Alfred Nobel,[1] the principles of neoclassical economics—in particular, the hypothesis that capital markets are efficient—have been applied to finance.

Do We Have a Science to Teach?

The first question is whether we have a science (or are making progress toward a science) to teach future investment professionals. Is our "science" merely an idealized rational construction that ignores market realities? If so, exactly what should we be teaching students of finance whose objective is to manage

---

[1]Hereafter called the "Nobel Prize in Economics." By spelling out the full name of the prize, we acknowledge that it was not in the list of prizes established by Alfred Nobel himself, but the Nobel Foundation clearly expresses its view that it is to be considered on an equal footing with the original Nobel prizes.

other people's money? Is an alternative science based on observations available (or in progress)? Or does our current knowledge of economics and finance have to be removed from the realm of science altogether and placed on a par with the social sciences?

In response to the criticisms leveled at mainstream finance theory following recurrent financial crises, the proponents of the theory defend its validity. They argue that all sciences use idealizations and that the idealizations used in mainstream economics and financial economics are useful, although they cannot foresee—or explain—financial crises such as the 2007–09 crash. According to mainstream theory, the cause of large market swings is attributable to exogenous events that the theory cannot predict.

Others consider crashes to be the consequence of random fluctuations in market returns. This view deserves explanation. The fact that a phenomenon can be described with simple probabilistic models does not *per se* preclude the existence of a deeper, more informative explanation of the same phenomenon. Different levels of explanation might coexist, of course, with different levels of accuracy. For example, random-number generators are perfectly deterministic models that generate sequences of numbers that appear to be random sequences. Finite sequences of numbers generated by random-number generators pass all tests of randomness and are described as sequences of independent draws from a given distribution. Although these sequences are generated by a deterministic model, they can be described with good approximation as random sequences.

In both the practice and the theory of finance, different families of statistical models of varying complexity can be used to describe the same data samples. The choice between these models is often based on statistical tests that do not allow any definitive answer. The possibility of describing crashes as random phenomena is not in contradiction with more refined models that have greater predictive power. By adopting appropriate distributions, one can take the simplified view that crashes are purely random events. This approach is the first level of approximation, the most coarse-grained view of market behavior. The theoretical challenge, however, is to find more informative explanations—in particular, explanations in which the conditional probability of market crashes depends on observed variables. This type of explanation is what is required from a *theory* of market crashes.

In his article "In Defence of the Dismal Science" (2009), which appeared on the *Economist* website on 6 August 2009, Robert Lucas, professor of economics at the University of Chicago and recipient of the 1995 Nobel Prize in Economics, wrote, "One thing we are not going to have, now or ever, is a set of models that forecast sudden falls in the value of financial assets, like the declines that followed the failure of Lehman Brothers in September [2008]."

This statement is somewhat misleading: It should be obvious that we are not going to have a *deterministic* model that predicts with certainty large market swings, their amplitude, and their timing. Rather what is expected of a scientific theory is that it allow to evaluate with reasonable accuracy the likelihood of a crisis.

In a glib dismal of the importance of the market crash, Robert Barro (2009), professor of economics at Harvard University, remarked during a roundtable discussion published two days later on the *Economist* website, "Economies have natural tendencies to recover from recessions, and such a recovery is the most likely outcome for the American economy going into 2010."

In our review of the literature following the 2007–09 financial crisis and in our conversations about the topic, one of the problems singled out with the prevailing theory as presently taught in most finance curricula is that the idealizations made by mainstream finance theory fail to take into account how real-world markets work. Mainstream academics are widely considered to be more interested in the quest for a unified theory than in understanding the workings of markets. For example, in the equity market, while mainstream academics often hold that stocks are priced correctly, there are, according to Dennis Logue, professor emeritus at the Tuck School of Business Administration at Dartmouth College and chairman of the board of directors of Ledyard Financial Group, "massive anomalies in the micro and macro sense."

Before discussing in more detail the defense and the critique of mainstream finance theory, we wish to briefly state what we mean by "mainstream" (or prevailing or dominant) because the term is subject to various interpretations. We use the term mainstream as shorthand for referring to the theory that is espoused in articles that appear in major journals and that is taught at major universities and business schools. We do not mean to suggest that every academic who might personally be considered mainstream adheres exactly to these views. The chief tenets of mainstream theory are (1) efficient markets, (2) rational expectations, and (3) optimization.

In the 1961–66 period, Jack Treynor, William Sharpe, John Lintner, and Jan Mossin independently introduced the first general equilibrium theory in finance, called the capital asset pricing model (CAPM). According to the CAPM, all agents share the same knowledge of the probability distributions of future returns and rely on mean–variance optimization to make their investment decisions. That is, all agents choose the optimal compromise between the expected return and the expected variance of their portfolio. As a result, they all invest in the same risky portfolio, the market portfolio. Their portfolios differ only in the amount allocated to cash (the "riskless" asset).

Robert Merton (1973), distinguished professor of finance at Sloan School of Management at the Massachusetts Institute of Technology (MIT) and a corecipient of the 1997 Nobel Prize in Economics, extended the CAPM in a dynamic environment in his seminal work. The Merton model is a multi-period model in which decisions are made by considering not only next-period returns but also the entire future price process of assets.

Mainstream economic theory developed in parallel with mainstream finance theory in the 1960s and 1970s in what is called the "rational expectations revolution." The starting point was the so-called Lucas critique. Professor Lucas observed that the estimation of the effect of changes in government policy is made ineffective by the fact that economic agents anticipate these changes and change their behavior. Therefore, he advocated giving a micro foundation to macroeconomics—that is, explaining macroeconomics in terms of the behavior of individual agents.

The result was a tendency in mainstream economic theory for macroeconomic models to be based on a multitude of agents characterized by rational expectations, optimization, and equilibrium. Mainstream finance theory uses the same basic structure as general equilibrium economics. It assumes markets are populated by a multitude of agents and each agent is identified by a utility function that assigns a numerical value to each possible investment choice. Each agent receives a stochastic (i.e., random) stream of endowments (i.e., exogenous positive cash flows). Endowments can represent any cash flow received outside of financial investments, such as salaries, gifts, or inheritances. At each trading moment, agents decide how much they want to consume, how much they want to invest in financial assets, and how much they want to keep as cash.

The principle of dynamic equilibrium in finance theory requires that at each moment, prices are such that the global demand for assets is equal to the global offer of assets. In the absence of arbitrage, the assumption is that all agents can be aggregated into a single representative agent. The consumption stream and the price process generated by this representative agent are the same as the aggregated consumption and relative price processes obtained by optimizing individual agents.

The assumptions made in mainstream finance theory are clearly unrealistic. So, is mainstream finance theory (or, generally, current mainstream macroeconomic theory) an empirical science at all in the modern sense? That is, is the theory based on observations?

Many would argue that financial economics does not belong to the realm of empirical science but to that of the social sciences. Michael Oliver, a senior lecturer in finance at the Open University and cofounder and director of Global Partnership Family Offices, remarked, "Economics is a social science, not a physical science."

The meaning behind this remark is that separating pure economics from political economics is difficult. In short, different economic theories correspond to different political choices. Economics and finance have as their subject an artifact, the economy or the markets, not laws of nature. The artifact is context specific: It is not independent of social or political objectives. Hence, separating empirical laws from statements of principles is not easy.

In his article "How Should the Financial Crisis Change How We Teach Economics?" (2010a), Robert Shiller, professor of economics at Yale University and a corecipient of the 2013 Nobel Prize in Economics, remarked on the number of critics of current mainstream economics. He concluded, "The reason there are such strong views about the profession going astray is that we do not have good scientific macroeconomic theories; we do not even have good ways of developing them" (p. 406).

Some have argued that the reason mainstream macroeconomics and mainstream finance theory are not scientific can be found in the design of these disciplines. John Kay, a distinguished British economist and visiting professor at the London School of Economics, observed that mainstream economics is a logical theory based on unrealistic assumptions without any consideration of real data. Professor Kay (2012) observed, "The distinguishing characteristic of [mainstream economists'] approach is that the list of unrealistic simplifying assumptions is extremely long" (p. 50). Discussing the ineffectiveness of policy—and, we might add, investment decisions—based on the assumptions of modern macroeconomics, Professor Kay went on to cite John Cochrane, professor of finance at the University of Chicago's Booth School of Business, who agrees that the assumptions used "are, as usual, obviously not true" (p. 51). That, Professor Kay remarked, would be the end of the discussion for any reasonable "scientist." Professor Cochrane argued, however, that "this [endlessly playing with unrealistic hypotheses] is exactly the right way of doing things." In the same article, Professor Kay commented on the absurdity that *a priori* deduction from a particular set of unrealistic simplifying assumptions is not simply a tool but, as stated by the University of Chicago's Gary Becker, winner of the 1992 Nobel Prize in Economics, "the heart of the economic approach" (p. 55).

Exhibit 1.1 summarizes the defense and some of the critiques of mainstream economic and finance theory and notes some elements that have been proposed that would characterize an alternative theory.

Exhibit 1.1. Defense and Critiques of Mainstream Economic and Finance Theory and Alternatives

Defense of Mainstream Finance Theory	Critique of Mainstream Finance Theory	Elements for an Alternative Theory
Mainstream finance theory is an idealized but valid representation of financial markets. Crises are unpredictable events and are subsequently self-correcting.	Mainstream finance theory models of rationality, agent independence, and equilibrium are unrealistic. Markets are neither stable nor self-regulating as held by equilibrium assumptions.	Markets are complex systems based on interacting (noncollapsible and not necessarily rational) agents. Markets are prone to crises because of aggregation phenomena. The money generation process is an essential component that leads to bubbles and crashes.

Poking Holes in the Theory

Mainstream finance theory is considered to be unrealistic not only because its main assumptions are unrealistic but also because the entire theoretical construction is not related to observable quantities. For example, such crucial data as future dividends and returns are not observable. In his book *Dynamics of Markets* (2009), University of Houston professor of physics Joseph McCauley noted,

> The idea of dividends and returns discounted infinitely into the future for financial assets is very shaky, because it makes impossible information demands on our knowledge of future dividends and returns. That is, it is impossible to apply with any reasonable degree of accuracy. (p. 65)

The fact that the theory makes impossible demands on our knowledge is a crucial point that affects all mainstream general equilibrium theories. Fundamental theoretical variables, such as prices, are defined as the discounted present value of an infinite stream of future quantities that are not observable.

Contrast this circumstance with physics, in which many theoretical terms are not directly observable but are defined through the theory itself. Consider temperature: We cannot directly observe temperature, which is a theoretical term interpreted as the amount of energy associated with the motion of certain molecules. All theoretical terms used to define temperature, however, are defined in function of observables. For example, suppose you measure the temperature of the body by using a clinical thermometer with a mercury column. What you actually observe is not temperature but the elongation of the mercury column. We translate the elongation of the mercury column into temperature because we have a global theory that links temperature with other observable characteristics such as *length* and *volume*. These terms are, indeed, observable. Thus, temperature can be defined, and it is a useful concept because it helps explain other observed phenomena.

Economic and finance theory, on the contrary, define terms in function of quantities that are not observable, nor can they be defined in function of observables. Quantities such as future dividends are not defined through a process of forecasting based on past data. If these terms were defined as a function of past data, then mainstream finance would be based on observable data. Mainstream finance, however, is based on future, clearly non-observable, data. In practice, any present value model of asset prices—that is, any model that says that today's price is based on discounted future cash flows—makes forecasts of unobservable future quantities.

In addition to this problem, which is fundamental, the critique of mainstream finance theory makes three key points that can be summarized as follows:

1. No real agent has a perfect knowledge of the future, not even in a probabilistic sense. Hence, the notion of rational expectations is unrealistic.

2. Because real agents have mutual interactions and are not coordinated solely by a central price signal, agents cannot be collapsed into a single representative agent.[2]

3. Economies are rarely in a state of equilibrium.

Alan Kirman (2009), professor emeritus of economics at the University of Aix-Marseille III and at the École des Hautes Études en Sciences Sociales, remarked,

> What has become the standard macroeconomic model . . . is justified by its proponents on the grounds that it . . . is based on rational maximising individuals. But there are two problems with this. . . . First, we have known since the mid-1970s that aggregating the behaviour of lots of rational individuals will not necessarily lead to behaviour consistent with that of some "representative agent". . . . Second, the axioms that are used to define "rationality" are based on the introspection of economists and not on the observed behaviour of individuals. (pp. 80–81)

---

[2]Neoclassical economics does not posit or require a representative agent but, instead, supposes that different agents will have different utility functions and that the market-clearing price will represent the net effects of all the agents in the market. In contrast, much of modern macroeconomics relies on a single representative agent. Without the assumption of a representative agent, the *dynamic stochastic general equilibrium models* most often used in macroeconomics are neither mathematically nor computationally tractable. There is no way to solve a dynamic stochastic optimization problem with a large number of independent utility functions.

How unrealistic are rational expectations? Eric Beinhocker (2007), executive director of the Institute for New Economic Thinking's research program at the University of Oxford (INET@Oxford), asked the reader to consider a rational agent who goes grocery shopping:[3]

> You have well-defined preferences for tomatoes compared with everything else you could possibly buy in the world, including bread, milk, and a vacation in Spain. Furthermore, you have well-defined preferences for everything you could possibly buy at any point in the future, and since the future is uncertain, you have assigned probabilities to those potential purchases. For example, I believe that there is a 23% chance that in two years, the shelf in my kitchen will come loose and I will need to pay $1.20 to buy some bolts to fix it. The discounted present value of that $1.20 is about $1.00, multiplied by a 23% probability, equals an expected value of 23 cents for possible future repairs, which I must trade off with my potential purchase of tomatoes today, along with all of my other potential purchases in my lifetime. . . . [To make your decisions,] you know exactly what your budget is for spending on tomatoes. To calculate this budget, you must have fully formed expectations of your future earnings over your entire lifetime and have optimized your current budget on the basis of that knowledge. In other words, you might hold back on those tomatoes because you know that the money spent on them could be better spent in your retirement. Of course, this assumes that your future earnings will be invested in a perfectly hedged portfolio of financial assets and that you take into account actuarial calculations on the probability that you will live until retirement at age 65, as well as your expectations of future interest rates, inflation, and the yen-to-dollar exchange rate. While standing there, staring at those nice, red tomatoes, you then feed all this information into your mind and perform a cunning and incredibly complex optimization calculation that trades off all these factors, and you come up with the perfectly optimal answer—to buy or not to buy! (p. 116)

This description might look like a caricature, but it is exactly what is implied by a rational expectations model.

According to the view of positive economics, mathematical models describe the outcome of financial decisions, not the process itself. This view, which says that the aggregate supply and demand is determined "as if" all these calculations took place, weakens the Lucas critique, which calls for a

---

[3]The Institute for New Economic Thinking (INET) is a not-for-profit think tank whose purpose is to support academic research and teaching in economics "outside the dominant paradigms of efficient markets and rational expectations." Founded in 2009 with the financial support of George Soros, INET is a response to the global financial crisis that started in 2007. For more information, see http://ineteconomics.org/.

microstructure foundation to macroeconomics, and is basically beyond any reasonable empirical test.

As for the second critique—that agents cannot be collapsed into a single representative agent—the Sonnenschein–Debreu–Mantel theorem (see Sonnenschein 1972) demonstrated that utility functions cannot be aggregated into the utility function of a single representative agent. The idea that agents have mutual interactions and are not coordinated solely by a central price signal was analyzed two decades ago by Professor Kirman (1992). Kirman (2010) subsequently wrote,

> [Macroeconomics is based on the assumption that] all that we have to do to deduce the behaviour of the economy at the aggregate, or macro, level is to add up the behaviour of the individuals who make it up. Furthermore, the theoretically unjustified assumption is made that the behaviour of the aggregate can be assimilated to that of an individual. (p. 501)

The critique that the representative agent is not a sound concept is based on the fact that one cannot aggregate utility functions and obtain a utility function with all the characteristics needed to justify equilibrium. Agents interact directly, for example, in herding behavior, as is well documented in the behavioral finance literature.

Paul Ormerod and Dirk Helbing (2012) wrote,

> We live now in a densely networked, strongly coupled, and largely interdependent world, which behaves completely differently from a system of independently optimizing decision makers. . . . The representative agent approach must be abandoned. . . . [It] cannot describe cascading effects well. These are determined not by the average stability, but by the weakest link. (p. 149)

As for the third critique—that markets are rarely in a state of equilibrium—critics of mainstream economic and finance theory point to the frequency and the magnitude of financial crises. At the 2013 International Monetary Fund (IMF) global economy forum, David Romer (2013), professor of political economy at University of California, Berkeley, remarked, "My view that we should think of financial shocks as closer to commonplace than to exceptional is based on history." Professor Romer counted six distinct shocks in US markets during the past 30 or so years that have posed important macroeconomic risks. Joseph Stiglitz (2013), professor of economics and University Professor at Columbia University and a corecipient of the 2001 Nobel Prize in Economics, counted approximately 100 financial crises worldwide in the past 30 years. Following closely on the 1987 stock market crash and 2000–01 bursting of the dot-com bubble, the most recent crisis has made it clear that tensions accumulate in economies and markets that lead to disequilibria and large market swings.

Completing the Theory

Mainstream economics and mainstream economists fail to recognize the existence of bubbles. In an interview, *New Yorker* columnist John Cassidy (2010) questioned Eugene Fama about efficient markets and the recent credit bubble in the US housing market. Professor Fama famously replied, "I don't know what a credit bubble means. I don't even know what a bubble means. These words have become popular. I don't think they have any meaning."

Nevertheless, attempts have been made to explain market bubbles and crashes within (or alongside) the existing theory. Among these are attempts to integrate into finance the consideration of liquidity, leverage, and other factors outside classical financial theory and to incorporate psychology (human behavior).

The Open University's Dr. Oliver commented on the importance of liquidity in explaining large stock market swings. He said,

> Until the financial crisis, the role of money was not taken seriously by most economists. Some economics models of the economy were even constructed without a banking system! The role of money (the term used by practitioners is "liquidity") needs to be reassessed.

Dr. Oliver collaborated with Gordon Pepper on the book *The Liquidity Theory of Asset Prices* (2006) and teaches the unit on liquidity during a two-day course titled "A Practical History of Financial Markets" at Edinburgh Business School.

The role of liquidity in the formation of sharp upward and downward market swings is now widely recognized, but will that recognition be enough to complete mainstream finance theory? Some sources we talked to are either not convinced that incorporating liquidity in asset-pricing models would improve our theory or models or consider it too early to tell. Sébastien Lleo, professor of finance at NEOMA Business School[4] (France) and visiting professor at the Frankfurt School of Finance and Management, cautioned, "We should be wary of claims that a single theory or tool can 'fix' our approach to finance. This will take a long time and require significant efforts."

A longer list of what is needed to rethink finance theory to take into consideration the real world was suggested by James Montier, a strategist with fund manager GMO. In his Manifesto for Change in his white paper "The Flaws of Finance" (2012), Mr. Montier suggested incorporating (together with liquidity) leverage, bad behavior, bad incentives, and delegated management.

---

[4]NEOMA Business School was formed by the recent merger of Rouen Business School and Reims Management School.

The role of human behavior in explaining large market swings has been explored by, among others, Professor Shiller. In his recent article "Bubbles Forever" (2013) on Project Syndicate, Professor Shiller suggested that bubbles might best be referred to as speculative epidemics: Enthusiasm spreads from person to person and, in the process, amplifies stories that might justify asset price increases. Shiller explored how psychological factors drive stock markets in his book *Irrational Exuberance*, first published in 2000 and updated in 2005.

Andrew Lo (2004), professor of finance and director of the Laboratory for Financial Engineering at MIT, developed what he calls the "adaptive market hypothesis." He argues that markets are not static but that they evolve continuously, not only under the pressure of exogenous events but also because of the competitive action of market participants. Professor Lo suggests that by applying the principles of evolution (competition, adaptation, and natural selection) to financial markets, we can explain the behavior of markets. In fact, he compares markets to ecologies competing for resources (i.e., profits). Market participants learn from experience and modify their forecasts and investment strategies to realize a gain. In competing for resources, the action of market participants tends to keep markets efficient while creating new opportunities for profit.

Note that, together with Lars Peter Hansen, professor of economics at the University of Chicago and a corecipient of the 2013 Nobel Prize in Economics, Professor Lo codirects the Macro Financial Modeling Group at the Becker Friedman Institute. The group consists of a network of macroeconomists working to develop improved models of the links between financial markets and the real economy in the wake of the 2007–09 financial crisis—a link that sources mentioned is lacking in today's theory.

One attempt to establish a historical link between the economy and markets (and predict the next growth cycle) was recently made by Hans-Joerg Naumer, head of capital markets and thematic research at Allianz Global Investors. Using the Russian economist Nikolai Kondratiev's theory of long waves of boom–bust business cycles and stock market data from Robert Shiller's *Irrational Exuberance* (2005) and Datastream, Mr. Naumer overlaid a rolling 10-year yield on the S&P 500 Index on Kondratiev's five long waves (see **Figure 1.1**).[5] Mr. Naumer's link is of an economic nature; that is, it associates long-term stock market trends with long business cycles. This link is different from the cycles implied by Minsky's financial instability hypothesis, which links the economy, financial markets, and the money generation process.

---

[5]Nikolai Dmitriyevich Kondratiev (or Kondratieff) was a Russian economist who lived from 1892 to 1938 and was known for his theory that Western capitalist economies have long-term (50–60 year) cycles characterized by successions of expansion and decline. These cycles are known as "Kondratiev waves." Kondratiev developed the theory in his 1925 book *The Major Economic Cycles*.

Figure 1.1. Kondratiev's Five Waves from 1780 to 2010 and the Rolling 10-Year Yield on the S&P 500

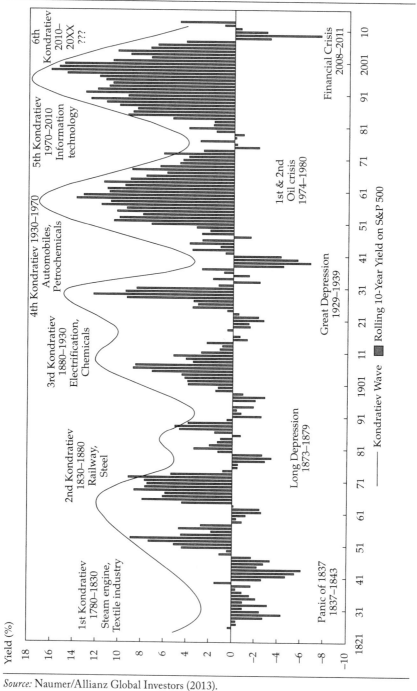

Source: Naumer/Allianz Global Investors (2013).

Finance Theory as Physics Envy

One might ask: Can the debate on the tenability of today's finance theory be resolved with the methods of empirical science? Will the debate remain at the level of dogma, as with the conflict between different views of political economics? Or will the debate remain at the epistemological level, centered on the question of what is the cognitive value of a model that, in the best case, captures only some general features of the real economy and real markets?

As mentioned previously, Lucas maintains that we will never have a set of models that forecasts sudden falls in the value of financial assets. He is referring to sure *deterministic* predictions. But mainstream economic and finance theories do make *probabilistic* predictions. The problem is that testing predictions is difficult when samples are small and noise abounds. In his famous paper "Noise," the late Fischer Black (1986) wrote, ". . . noise makes it very difficult to test either practical or academic theories about the way that financial or economic markets work. We are forced to act largely in the dark" (p. 529).

Do we have a science? Would you feel safe flying if you knew that there were linear differential equations that describe an airplane's structure but that no such equations can be identified? The abstract mathematical knowledge that structures can be described by linear differential equations allows one to neither engineer nor study any real structure. Yet, this knowledge is the knowledge embedded in general equilibrium models.

One objection to this critique is that we *can* have an understanding of economics that cannot be formalized in a mathematical model. This objection is likely to be true—the Wright brothers, who were bicycle mechanics, designed their planes "as if" they had the mathematical knowledge of the structure—but the objection does not lend any support to mainstream models. If we can describe economic behavior without models, we do not need general equilibrium theories.

Ultimately, the debate on general equilibrium models in economics and finance theory may be empty. Clearly, general equilibrium models are not empirically validated in terms of the characteristics and interactions of real agents. Given any asset-pricing model that does not admit arbitrage, however, we can always formulate an equivalent abstract general equilibrium model.

In classical physics, the laws of motion can be expressed either through differential equations or through the minimization of a functional, the Hamiltonian or the Lagrangian.[6] The predictive power of physics depends on the fact that we know how to write Hamiltonian and Lagrangian terms. The mere existence of a Hamiltonian functional does not, however, add to our understanding of a physical phenomenon.

---

[6]This statement refers to a purely mathematical fact. The differential equations of dynamics can be obtained as the solution of a maximization problem.

In finance theory, we do not know how to describe a representative agent based on empirical data, nor can we empirically ascertain the functional form of a representative agent for large markets. The pure mathematical existence of an abstract mathematical representative agent does not add much to our economic understanding of financial markets.

Consider the simplest general equilibrium model, the capital asset pricing model (CAPM). Given a set of expected returns, we can always think of these expected returns as generated by the CAPM. This pure mathematical abstraction is always true. Of course, real agents do not behave as prescribed by the CAPM. In addition, if we go beyond a single period, which is the time horizon of the CAPM, then its predictions are no longer valid. We can always find a dynamic version of a general equilibrium model, however, that can generate any stream of returns. The problem is that we have no way to actually estimate such a model from empirical data.

We explore the implications of these ideas on the teaching of finance in Chapter 3.

As for the theory and the actual practice in investment management in the postcrisis period, Jaap van Dam, head of strategy and research at the Dutch pension fund PGGM (with more than €131 billion in assets under management), remarked,

> More than in changing the [prevailing] tenets themselves, their application in investment management is changing and they are being complemented with empirical analysis and common sense. What we need to reconsider is the universal applicability of these tenets and to admit their inherent limitations. A theory is just a theory. A typical formulation of a theory is of the type "if X, then Y." Understanding the limitations of the "if X" part has probably become more important. This applies to theories like CAPM, for example, which is now best viewed as an idealized model.

Commenting on market equilibria and typical no-arbitrage assumptions, Steven Greiner, director of portfolio risk at FactSet Research Systems, remarked, "[These] are not so relevant as professors think for the practice of asset management. It is enough to know that efficiency rises with liquidity and that mispricing is empirically demonstrable."

Finance as a Social Science?

If prevailing theory indeed fails to represent the world as it is and has effectively proved to be of little *practical* use, can we consider our economic and finance theory to be hard science? Wouldn't it be better to reinstate economics and finance as social sciences, albeit quantitative social sciences (given the inherently quantitative nature of the data), and allot a reduced role to the complex mathematics and modeling (in light of the problems with the theory behind the math)?

Dr. Oliver remarked,

> Over the past 20 years I have watched in despair as universities and business schools have grilled students with existence theorems and trained them to be competent as mathematicians, frequently at the expense of understanding how the real-world macroeconomy works.

Two arguments can be raised against considering economic/finance theory to be a mathematical science. The first is that economics and finance are dominated by single events that cannot be predicted or even described in mathematical terms. Nassim Taleb, professor of risk engineering at Polytechnic Institute of New York University and author of *The Black Swan* (2010), advocates this view. He popularized the notion of "black swans," unpredictable events that change the course of an economy and that are wrongly rationalized after they occur.

The key question is not whether unpredictable events occur. Of course, they do. In corporate finance, some decisions made by senior managers are difficult to model. In political economics, some key decisions made by heads of states or central banks are difficult to predict. Changes in the behavior of masses—such as herding, which changes the demand for an entire market—are also difficult to predict. The crucial question is whether these events can be handled with statistical techniques or whether the complexity of the economic system makes individual events critical for the future development of an economy or markets and thus not susceptible to statistical treatment.

The second argument in favor of considering finance to be more a social science than a physical science is that the dynamics of economic and financial phenomena are simply too complex to be captured by mathematical formulas—at least with today's mathematics. Or perhaps the phenomena are too complex to allow a parsimonious mathematical description. But this characteristic, the proponents of a reduced role for mathematics argue, does not imply that we cannot make empirically meaningful economic statements outside a mathematical model. This camp observes that economic thinking existed well before the mathematization of economics and finance. Basic economic ideas can be explained in plain English, and reasoning on economic and financial facts can be done without formulas.

Russell Napier, a consultant with CLSA Asia-Pacific Markets and author of *The Anatomy of the Bear: Lessons from Wall Street's 4 Great Bottoms* (2005) argued,

> Finance is all about establishing value. To do so, we need a better understanding of humans, we need to remove finance from the field of science and place it more in sociology. Sociology today cannot be used as a predictive force but a field for learning. Sometime in the future, finance might migrate back to being a science. But, we cannot afford to have more theoretical *culs*

de sac. We cannot afford more problems deriving from the spurious certainties often inherent in the pricing of derivatives.

Similar views have been expressed by others. For example, British economist John Kay (2012) wrote,

> Economic behavior is influenced by technologies and cultures, which evolve in ways that are certainly not random but which cannot be described fully, or perhaps at all, by the kinds of variables and equations with which economists are familiar. (p. 52)

Whether we view our economic and finance theory as a hard science or as a social science influences what we teach, which we explore in Chapter 3.

Commenting on the present-day emphasis on mathematics in finance programs, Dr. Oliver remarked,

> Many of the recently introduced programs at business schools and universities with a concentration in mathematical finance are divorced from events in the real world. We are producing economists who can give you an equation for everything but who lack any broader knowledge. Economics is a social science and not a physical science, and as such, it needs to refocus on core social science values.

Even proponents of the use of models in investment management caution about their use. Professor Lleo remarked,

> For me the problem is not the application of mathematics in areas where we do not have a strong theory. This is rather healthy: We need models—mathematical, philosophical, sociological—to act as frames of reference if we are to tackle any significant question. The real problem is the application of mathematics in areas where we *do have* a strong theory. Our financial economic theory makes strong assumptions to derive strong results. The problem is that these assumptions are often unrealistic. However, we often lose sight of this fact because of the appeal and apparent universality of the "strong theory" we have developed. The existence of a strong prescriptive or normative theory necessarily generates overconfidence and leads to the application of the wrong type of conceptual tool, be it mathematical or sociological.

Professor Lleo cited as an example the pricing of collateralized debt obligations (CDOs), for which, he said, we do have a strong theory (no-arbitrage pricing via hedging/replication) that enabled us in the past to use advanced mathematics confidently. Unfortunately, he added, "The structure and nature of CDOs did not satisfy the fundamental assumptions, which led to disaster."

Can we have meaningful empirical knowledge even when mathematical modeling is not possible? The answer is clearly yes. For example, we can describe fairly well, in plain English, the process of the growth of a tree even if we do not have a detailed mathematical description of the growth of trees. Generally, we can say that many levels of description of phenomena are possible. We have many levels of "coarse graining" in mathematical descriptions, but in addition, we have descriptions in natural languages that, although less precise than mathematical descriptions, are still meaningful.

Forcing mathematization can actually impoverish, not enrich, knowledge. The imposition of a mathematical language may make important facts impossible to convey. Professor Lleo believes that economic thinking became poorer in some aspects just as it was becoming more structured and precise in others. He cites the work of Frank Knight (1921), who introduced the distinction between risk and uncertainty, and of John Maynard Keynes (1936), who introduced the notion of "animal spirits." "Yet," Professor Lleo commented, "finance theory tells us a different story: Uncertainty can be viewed as idiosyncratic risk and diversified away. The only source of return should be related to market risk premia and the scaling of risk exposure."

More than Simply a Social Science?

Although some argue that economics and finance should be considered social sciences, others argue for stricter adherence to the paradigm of empirical science. Again, the impact on the curriculum is not negligible.

The discussion of the role of mathematics in scientific enquiry is not new: The entire development of science was marked by a debate on the use of mathematics. Galileo Galilei was the first to state that science was inherently mathematical. In his *The Assayer*, Galileo (1623) wrote,

> [The Book of Nature] . . . is written in the language of mathematics, and its characters are triangles, circles, and other geometrical figures, without which it is humanly impossible to understand a single word of it; without these, one is wandering around in a dark labyrinth.

This statement was prophetical but in advance of its time: With the mathematics known to Galileo, one could not have formulated modern physics. Only later, with the development of calculus by Gottfried Leibnitz and Sir Isaac Newton, did mathematics acquire the tools for formulating mechanical laws in mathematical terms. The publication of Newton's *Principia Mathematica* in 1687 marked the beginning of modern mathematical science. The mathematics of calculus—in particular, differential equations that link variables with their rate of change—proved to be a powerful concept in all scientific disciplines.

Still, prior to the invention of computers, the practical application of mathematics was limited to establishing general properties, such as the existence of solutions of differential equations, and finding closed-form solutions of differential equations. Thus, many problems in empirical science were not formalized mathematically. For example, empirical problems related to weather forecasts, biology, botany, hydrology, even the design of mechanical structures, were not fully formalized. Nevertheless, these problems are part of empirical science. Quantitative laws did apply, but they were far from providing a full mathematical description of these phenomena. Often, the solution to engineering problems continued to require human judgment.

The introduction of high-performance computers marked a new epoch in the application of mathematics to science and engineering and ushered in the application of computational mathematics. Fast computers allowed the simulation of phenomena. Instead of being limited to closed-form solutions of differential equations, analysts have been able to actually create, through simulation, structures of numbers or symbols that mimic the structure of reality. This ability greatly increased the number of areas for the practical applicability of mathematics. Today, we can simulate with amazing accuracy the behavior of large-scale objects, such as airplanes, or natural events, such as tornados, and possibly, because the use of mathematics in science is subject to evolution, reproduce some human cognitive functions.

Many complex phenomena, however, remain beyond the ability of detailed mathematical representation, and for various reasons—including chaos and sensitivity to initial conditions, objective complexity (the extent to which the phenomenon is close to randomness), and because we do not know the laws. But these are moving targets. For example, because of improved computers and software, weather forecasting has become progressively more accurate, but as we all have noticed, it can still be wide of the mark. Professor Logue compared our ability to forecast using our economic and finance theory with the ability of a meteorologist. He remarked,

> Our inability to forecast is a "super problem." As with the weather system, it is very difficult to identify where we are now and even more difficult to identify where we will be in the future. We have all heard the local radio weatherman say 60% chance of rain while at the same time looking out the window at a deluge.

David Colander, professor of economics at Middlebury College, Vermont, gave the argument a twist. He remarked (2009), "The problem is not that economics is too mathematical; it is that the mathematics we use in economics is way too simple to capture the complexities of economic interrelationships" (p. 12).

Others agree and have argued that this situation calls for greater use of reasoning in managing assets. Edward Qian, chief investment officer (CIO) and head of multiasset research at PanAgora, said that the ability to reason on issues in finance and economics is what is critical; mathematics provides a tool for reasoning. He commented,

> Finance is based on powerful ideas and insights about the market, it is not based on powerful mathematics. But as the field evolves, it seems it has

shifted to more mathematics and more sophisticated models. In doing so, it is easy to forget the underlying assumptions, some of which are highly unrealistic. In recent years, students with a strong mathematics and computer science background, who would have gone to mathematics and science programs, are recruited to finance and economic graduate programs. But only those who can think deeply and independently about issues in finance and economics can be expected to become successful investors.

Clearly, in some domains of empirical science, all-encompassing mathematical formulations are not possible. Economics and financial economics are probably only partially susceptible to mathematical theories. Although mathematical reasoning is useful, it probably has to be complemented with less formal reasoning: Important single events occur that we do not know how to describe mathematically but we can rationalize. This circumstance limits but does not exclude the use of mathematics in economics and finance. For example, we might not have a lot of data on rare events, such as market crashes and depressions, but we can formulate reasonable scenarios for such events that can, in turn, be mathematically represented.

Critics of economics and finance as a mathematical science are probably right in saying that these fields cannot be completely represented as unified mathematical theory. To deny that some parts of economic theories can be mathematically described, however, would be unscientific.

Finance as an Empirical Science

Treating economics and finance more as social sciences is one alternative to prevailing practice. Stricter adherence to the paradigm of empirical science is the other. We will refer generally to this latter approach as "scientific economics" or "scientific finance."

We can broadly distinguish three main subfields of scientific economics: (1) econometrics and signal processing applied to financial economics, (2) statistical mechanics applied to financial economics, and (3) the theory of complex systems and network theory.

Econometrics is the oldest application of scientific principles to economics and finance. It is based on applying statistical methods—in particular, time-series analysis—to empirical data. The diffusion of electronic transactions and the consequent availability of high-frequency and tick-by-tick data have enabled new methods of time-series analysis borrowed from the field of signal processing.

Techniques such as econometrics and signal processing can be considered applications of the scientific method in restricted domains in investment management, such as trading and execution. These techniques are based on collecting data, constructing hypothetical models, and then testing the models. The key problem with econometrics and signal processing is the amount of noise in empirical finance data, which makes estimates highly uncertain. The choice of model is rarely based on compelling data.

The application of statistical mechanics to financial economics is a new field. Of the results obtained, perhaps the best known is the celebrated presence of "fat tails" in most economic data distributions. The presence of fat tails in distributions implies that large events have a nonnegligible probability of happening. In a Gaussian distribution, on the contrary, large events—say, those more than three standard deviations from the mean of the distribution—can be safely ignored. Not so with fat-tailed, non-Gaussian distributions. Fat tails play a fundamental role in investment management, with important implications for the notion of diversification, risk–return optimization, and risk management.

The discovery that economic and financial variables are not Gaussian but exhibit fat tails is a cornerstone of modern financial modeling. The modeling of fat tails with stable distributions and their application to finance is a major innovation. Fifty years ago, Benoit Mandelbrot (1963) provided the first fundamental attack on the assumption that price or return distributions are normally distributed. His empirical evidence, based on various time series of commodity returns and interest rates, strongly rejected normality as a distributional model for asset returns. Instead, Mandelbrot conjectured that financial returns are more appropriately described by a non-normal stable distribution. Supported by the work of Fama (1963a, 1963b), this result led to a consolidation of the hypothesis that asset returns can be better described as a stable Paretian distribution.

Svetlozar Rachev, professor at Stony Brook University, New York; Christian Menn of the University of Applied Sciences in Mainz, Germany; and Frank Fabozzi, co-author of this book, outlined the disruptive impact of stable distributions on financial modeling in their book *Fat-Tailed and Skewed Asset Return Distributions* (2005). As they noted, the findings of Mandelbrot and Fama caused considerable concern in the finance profession. The authors quoted Paul Cootner (1964), a highly regarded financial economist who taught at both MIT and Stanford, who noted that if financial and economic variables were confirmed to follow a stable distribution, "almost without exception, past econometric work is meaningless" (p. 337). Cootner went on to warn that before the Paretian hypothesis about asset returns should be accepted, more evidence was needed.

As Rachev et al. (2005) noted, however, although a preponderance of empirical evidence was against normal distribution and supported fat-tailed distributions of financial variables, the "normality" assumption remained the cornerstone of many leading theories used in finance. In fact, the authors argued, the highly innovative nature of describing financial variables with stable distributions led to a rejection of these distributions, often on the basis of very weak arguments. For example, a strong objection was that there is no closed-form representation of stable distributions, an objection that the diffusion of powerful computers and numerical methods has made obsolete.

In addition to the fat-tailed nature of financial phenomena, any empirically based model must take into consideration the fundamental self-referentiality of financial markets and the models we use. Professor Lleo commented,

> Any model, field, or theory has a sociological dimension. Models are reflective, in the sense that a model that is widely adopted will tend to perform better and better, which in turn speeds up its adoption. This feedback loop can also turn against the model, as we have seen with value at risk [VaR] during the crisis: If all market participants adopt the same set of standards then they will tend to behave homogenously, which speeds up the growth of a bubble and precipitates market crises.

Why Are Mainstream Economic and Financial Economic Theories So Resilient?

Despite the failings in practical applications and numerous studies that show how unrealistic the assumptions are, mainstream economic and finance theories are remarkably resilient. One explanation is that general equilibrium theories embody the notion of economic rationality. From the point of view of economists, rationality has many advantages. It allows the creation of a sophisticated theoretical construction even when data are missing or difficult to interpret.

Benjamin Friedman (2010) professor of political economy at Harvard University, wrote,

> It sometimes seems that many economists write, and teach, not about the world in which we live but rather the world in which they wished we lived—perhaps because the alternative world is analytically easier to handle, or perhaps because they find the policy implications that would follow in that world more to their liking, or perhaps for yet other reasons. This path is very seductive. Especially in the intellectual arena, few ideas offer more appeal than a model that is simple, elegant, and wrong. (p. 3 of electronic document)

MIT's Professor Lo (2012) suggests that economists suffer from theory envy; that is, their objective is to create a structure that is on a par with their colleagues in the physical sciences. In commenting on the "exalted role of theory in economics," Professor Lo wrote, "Theoretical foundations have become a hallmark of economics, making it unique among the social sciences, but any virtue can become a vice when taken to the extreme of theory envy." (p. 45)

Neoclassical economists defend general equilibrium as an idealized framework that represents an economy without the imperfections of real economies; that is, the model is correct and reality is wrong. In finance theory, which has adopted the principles of classical economics, including general equilibrium, the real-world behavior of prices is said to present "price anomalies."

However, another powerful motivation exists: Economic rationality includes faith in the optimality of markets and their self-correcting capability. In his *History of Economics*, John Kenneth Galbraith (1987) remarked that economic theory reflects the ideology of the dominating power. For example, the Iron Law of Wages was described in the early nineteenth century by the English banker and economist David Ricardo. Ricardo considered that wages "naturally" tended toward a minimum level—the price that would allow laborers to subsist and perpetuate without increase or diminution in their number. For factory owners in an industrializing Great Britain, the idea was quite attractive. Unfortunately, for those same factory owners, Ricardo's "labor theory of value," as he called it, also influenced Marx in his early pessimistic views about the possibility that workers might benefit from capitalism. The rest is history.

The fact that theory reflects the interests of the dominating power is not limited to economics. In Renaissance France, as the power of French kings was being consolidated, French jurist and political philosopher Jean Boudin put forward a theory of sovereignty that argued in favor of absolutism as the best political system.

Thomas Kuhn (1962) analyzed the path through which science makes progress. According to Kuhn's classical analysis, science starts with the accumulation of data and empirical evidence. The tendency is always to defend current theories, grudgingly making adjustments when the theory is no longer tenable, but the accumulation of new empirical evidence can force a paradigm shift that results in new competing theories.

Kuhn observed that science, like economic and political theory, is not neutral: Political and ideological influences shape its development. Of several well-known examples, an often cited one comes from the Soviet Union, where the ideas of the biologist and agronomist Trofim Lysenko were imposed in the Stalin era even though they were plainly wrong. Lysenko rejected Mendelian genetics in favor of the hybridization theories of the Russian horticulturist Ivan V. Michurin.[7] Lysenko argued that crops' inheritance was environmentally acquired. Scientific dissent from Lysenko's theory was formally outlawed in 1948. As a result, Soviet research in biology came to a virtual halt

---

[7]Gregor Mendel was a central European monk and teacher of mathematics, physics, and Greek. He used the microscope to conduct research on the basic facts of heredity. In his research on the common pea plant, Mendel discovered that certain traits show up in offspring without any blending of parent characteristics. The mechanisms of heredity that he discovered working on plants are basically the same for all complex forms of life. Michurin was one of the founding fathers of scientific agricultural selection. He worked on hybridization of plants of similar and different origins. The most important problems elaborated by him were intervarietal and distant hybridization.

and programs to improve agricultural output fell far short of their objectives. After 1965, when Lysenko lost all political support, official sanction was bestowed on the view that Michurin was a breeder of genius whose unusual methods can be explained by genetics.

Following a series of economic and financial crises that have made it difficult to maintain intact mainstream theories of equilibrium and rational agents, economic and finance theory also might be moving toward a turning point. Many are now calling for modification of the prevailing paradigm or even a paradigm change. But changing a scientific paradigm is never easy. Max Planck (1949 or 1950), a founder of quantum mechanics, wrote, "A new scientific truth does not triumph by convincing its opponents and making them see the light, but rather because its opponents eventually die, and a new generation grows up that is familiar with it." Or, as he put it more succinctly: "Science advances one funeral at a time."

Yet another explanation is that mainstream economists and financial economists dominate the major publications and have created an effective barrier to the publication of ideas critical of or challenging mainstream theory. Professor Kay (2012) commented on the difficulty of getting published if one does not adhere to mainstream neoclassical thinking.[8] He said,

> You would be told that your model was theoretically inadequate: It lacked rigour, failed to demonstrate consistency. You might be accused of the cardinal sin of being "ad hoc." Rigour and consistency are the two most powerful words in economics today. . . . [Consistency and rigour] have undeniable virtues, but for economists they have particular interpretations. Consistency means that any statement about the world must be made in the light of a comprehensive descriptive theory of the world. Rigour means that the only valid claims are logical deductions from specified assumptions. Consistency is, therefore, an invitation to ideology, rigour an invitation to mathematics. (p. 52)

Other sources have commented on the difficulty of getting published in major professional publications for anything other than what supports the

---

[8]By "mainstream neoclassical thinking," we mean so-called freshwater economics based on the theories of bounded rationality, the efficient market hypothesis, and rational expectations. This school of thought is often referred to as "freshwater economics" because its major proponents, including Lucas and Fama, come from universities in or near the Great Lakes region, such as the University of Chicago and Carnegie Mellon. The school of thought based on Keynesian economics places less emphasis on theoretical and model consistency and considers examples of irrational behavior interesting and important. This school of thought is often referred to as "saltwater economics" because its major proponents, including Shiller and Lo, come from universities on the east and west coasts of the United States, such as Yale, MIT, and the University of California, Berkeley. A new synthesis of the two is referred to as "brackish-water economics."

prevailing economic and finance theory. Bruce Jacobs, principal of Jacobs Levy Equity Management, said:

> Conflicts of interest in the rarified world of professional publications may seem like an arcane concern, unlikely to have much influence on the real world. But conflicts of interest can lead to self-referential, closed systems that discourage learning and growth. The more closed a system of thinking becomes, the more defensive it is toward criticism, the tighter it holds onto its beliefs, and the less able it is to recognize its own faults. A positive feedback system is created, in which only affirmation of already held opinions is permitted. Conflict-of-interest standards can weaken the defenses that protect such a faulty system.

Indeed, many researchers wanting to publish findings that poke holes in the prevailing theory cannot get published in major economic and finance journals. Most papers that explore new ideas outside the framework of mainstream neoclassical economic and finance theory have been published in such journals as *Nature* or *Physica*.[9]

What is, perhaps, more disturbing is that mainstream journals reject papers that present empirical results and statistical analyses unless the findings are in line with mainstream theory. The accumulation of empirical results is fundamental, however, for the progress of any empirical science. In the hard sciences, from physics to biology, if reported results do not fit existing theories, the results are first verified by other researchers and, if confirmed, a process of theory revision starts. In economics and financial economics, results that do not fit the theory are often simply ignored or are considered anomalies, making mainstream theory virtually unassailable and resistant to change.

The internet, however, may be changing this situation. At least, such is the (optimistic) view of Andrew Haldane (2012), executive director for financial stability of the Bank of England. He remarked that academia's way of "keeping score" looked "increasingly antiquated." He wrote,

> Journal publication remains the main currency, but it is a devalued currency, at least as a medium of exchange for ideas. Some of the top names in the economics world have taken to social media and the blogosphere to propagate their ideas. This has the benefit not just of immediacy but reach. It amounts to using those network externalities to academic advantage. (p. 139)

In summary, mainstream economics and financial economics are not empirical sciences in the sense that physics and chemistry are: Many of the terms used are meaningless; assumptions are unrealistic; and the theory cannot be validated with empirical tests. Despite this empirical failure, mainstream neoclassical theories remain the prevailing theoretical model.

---

[9]*Physica* is a journal published by Elsevier consisting of subjournals A through E, of which A and E publish peer-reviewed research on econophysics.

The most recent crisis, however, has allowed critics to gain a hearing; new ideas—either more scientific, in that they are based on empirical data, or on the contrary, arguing that economics and finance should be placed back in the realm of the social sciences—are beginning to be discussed seriously.

As Professor Lo (2012) wrote:

> The recent financial crisis has exposed some serious gaps in our understanding of the global economy, and the need to take stock and get our academic house in order has never been greater. This presents us with a precious opportunity to make wholesale changes to our discipline that would otherwise be impossible, so we should delay no longer. (p. 48)

2. The Theory and Practice of Investment Management after the Crisis: Need for Change?

In the previous chapter, we explored some of the problems with mainstream or classical finance and economics. Continuing to base our discussion on a review of the literature and conversations with finance professionals in academia and the industry, we now consider whether and how the theory and practice of investment management *as taught (and practiced) today* needs to be revisited.

As discussed in the preceding chapter, current mainstream finance theory is embodied in general equilibrium models. These models are idealized mathematical representations of an economy and markets populated by rational agents who have perfect knowledge of all possible contingencies now and into the infinite future and who optimize the utility derived from consumption and production. Agents are coordinated by price signals. The capital asset pricing model is the prototype of general equilibrium models.

As noted in Chapter 1, even many of the theory's advocates acknowledge that these models are unrealistic (or simplistic) and require additional "pieces." Real agents do not have rational expectations; they interact and cannot be collapsed into a single representative agent.

More serious, perhaps, from the point of view of science, is that general equilibrium models cannot be estimated from empirical data. In particular, the utility function of the representative agent cannot be estimated; that is, general equilibrium models cannot be validated. They offer an idealized representation of financial markets and economies at large that does not take into consideration such fundamental elements as the banking system, liquidity, employment and wages, instabilities due to cascades of interactions, and crises. Work is being done to add some of these and other components to the theory. But many are now questioning whether financial economics *can* be reduced to a global model, useful as such a model might be.

So, do the theory and practice of investment need to be revisited? Didier Sornette, a physicist by training and chair of Entrepreneurial Risks at ETH Zurich, summed up the feeling of many of the individuals we talked to for this study. He said,

> The crash of 2008 certainly put on the radar screen many of the problems with traditional finance. But so did the LTCM [Long-Term Capital

Management] crisis in 1998, and so did many other crises. There is a strong incentive in the business to forget lessons.

We will now explore some of those lessons with a bearing on the teaching and practice of investment management, namely:

- diversification,

- optimization—diversification formalized,

- the CAPM and similar models,

- the efficient market hypothesis,

- risk measurement and risk management, and

- crises.

For each of these topics, after a brief review of the theoretical framework, we present the various opinions and conclude with proposals for change.

Diversification

Since the pioneering work of Harry Markowitz (1952), diversification has been a fundamental concept in asset management and asset-pricing theories. The notion of diversification can be traced back to medieval merchants and perhaps to well before the Greco-Roman world.[10] The concept is so essential that it has been popularized by the adage: "Don't put all your eggs in one basket." In finance, diversification implies that you can obtain the same expected returns but reduce your risk by investing in a portfolio of many assets rather than investing in only one or a few assets.

From a statistical point of view, diversification is summarized in two mathematical facts: (1) by appropriately choosing weights—that is, the proportion of funds invested in each asset—one can reduce the variance of a portfolio while maintaining unchanged its expected return and (2) the minimum possible variance of a portfolio is smaller than the variance of any of its components.

---

[10]For example, the rabbinical writings of medieval Judaism (e.g., the Talmud) emphasize diversification explicitly. A well-known piece of advice is to keep one-third of one's fortune in business, one-third in land, and one-third "at hand." Some have said that the Greco-Roman world did not have a notion of risk because Greeks and Romans believed that the Gods and the Fates determine human fortunes. This conclusion is questionable in light of the high place reserved for "Prudence" in the hierarchy of Greco-Roman virtues. In fact, in antiquity, Prudence was represented as the two-faced god Janus—one face old, the other young because the Ancients believed that Prudence was acquired by consideration of the past and foresight of the future: Does this sound like risk management? Note that Janus was a remote god considered to have rescued men from savagery. Moreover, the ancient Greeks entered into insurance contracts, which are also mentioned in the earlier (1770 BCE) Code of Hammurabi in what is now Iraq.

Because it allows one to reduce variance without affecting returns, diversification has often been described as the "only free lunch in financial markets."[11] If, for example, stocks and their returns are uncorrelated and individual variances bounded, then the variance of a portfolio can be made arbitrarily small by increasing the number of stocks. Stock returns are correlated, however, so diversification has lower bounds. In fact, market-wide correlation implies the existence of common factors that affect the entire market.[12] This is the celebrated separation between diversifiable risk—that is, risk that can be diversified away—and nondiversifiable risk.

These properties are purely statistical facts and are, of course, undisputed. What has been questioned is the *applicability* of diversification. In fact, in the 2007–09 financial crisis, portfolios that were supposed to be well diversified and, therefore, protected from the risk of large losses actually lost significant value. For example, those invested in the S&P 500, which is, in itself, highly diversified (but consisting entirely of equities), would have lost 57% from the market's peak (9 October 2007) to its bottom (9 March 2009).

Doubts have been voiced as to the effectiveness of diversification at every level of aggregation. Evariste Lefeuvre (2012), CIO and chief economist for the Americas at Natixis Global Asset Management, commented, "Recent empirical analysis shows that expanding the asset mix to [include more] equity-like assets [as well as equities *per se*] does not provide the expected benefits of asset allocation (the so-called 'only free lunch' in finance)" (p. 17).

Nevertheless, defenders of diversification argue that diversification always "works" if we define the opportunity set of asset classes broadly enough. The argument is that it is not economically possible for all asset classes to go down together. When "everybody" sells something, they buy something else and whatever they are buying goes up if we expand sufficiently the asset classes. Critics of this claim argue, however, that in a severe crisis, all production and commercial activities can be impaired and the total value of investable assets can go down.

Exhibit 2.1 summarizes the defense and critique of diversification according to our conversations with the industry and academic sources and a review of the literature.

---

[11]Diversification is not really a free lunch if assets are priced as if investors are already diversified. In such a condition, which seems likely to be true, *not* to diversify is wasteful (throwing away one's lunch). There is no such thing as a free lunch. Nevertheless, it is sometimes pedagogically useful to refer to diversification in such terms.

[12]This statement is not rigorous and would need appropriate mathematical qualifications. Empirical correlations might appear to be random fluctuations of a random matrix, and correlations might affect only some sectors and not the entire market.

Exhibit 2.1.   The Defense and Critique of Diversification

Defense of Diversification	Critique of Diversification
Diversification is a sound statistical concept that can be fully applied to protect against diversifiable risk. Loss of effectiveness of diversification is the result of unpredictable random fluctuations.	The application of diversification, in itself a sound statistical concept, is limited by changes in the parameters of the economy and by nonlinearity and nonnormality. In some economic states, diversification works well; in others, much less so because most returns are negative. For diversification to work correctly, regime shifts must be predicted and diversification adapted to changing regimes.

In other words, the defenders of diversification argue that, although it might occasionally fail because of random fluctuations of market parameters, diversification remains a major component of investment decision making. To be maximally effective, however, diversification requires the stability of parameters, covariances, and expected returns. In practice, these parameters change and limit the effectiveness of diversification. Critics argue that diversification is ineffective in many economic states, such as when large market swings or crashes occur. A sound use of diversification would imply, therefore, forecasting the regime shifts between economic states.

Note that this debate is part of a broader debate between the proponents of the "rationality of markets" and its critics. Proponents of market rationality believe that large (negative) market swings or crashes are an expression of the business cycle and markets' random behavior—that is, local events in which asset value is lost but subsequently (rapidly) recovered. Let's now consider the various issues and points of view related to diversification.

Mainstream economic and finance theory are equilibrium theories. Although, theoretically, fundamentals may change and produce long-lasting recessions and crises, barring significant exogenous events such as wars, the slow change of fundamentals can be foreseen in the classical framework and corrective measures can be implemented. The neoclassical framework does not disregard risk, but risk is exogenous in that framework.

The defenders of the neoclassical framework argue that diversification is a sound concept. Occasional failures of diversification are not the expression of structural change but result because correlations are stochastic in nature and, therefore, vary randomly. Barton Waring, former CIO for investment strategy and policy of Barclays Global Investors, now active as a writer and lecturer on those topics, commented that after the 2008 stock market crash, people said that the risk models had failed as correlations went to 1. But, he said,

> This occasional happenstance that correlations go toward 1 is actually perfectly normal. Consider, for example, a 100-year history of two series with a low correlation, created using simulation methods. So, the overall

correlation is perfectly as expected, but if you examined three-year subperiods, you would see a great deal of variability [in correlation], with some subperiods approaching a correlation of 1, and some approaching zero. Time-varying correlations over the shorter term are perfectly normal even for series that have a rock-solid longer term correlation relationship.

Mr. Waring argues that the risk models did not fail. They probably simply experienced normal correlation variability.

In addition to the stochastic nature of the covariance matrix, defenders of diversification point out that diversification works only for idiosyncratic risk. It cannot protect against factor-related risk. They observe that investors have to be realistic about the limits of diversification: It cannot protect against the risk associated with common factors. As the proportion of nondiversifiable risk increases, diversification becomes less effective.

Paul Pfleiderer (2012), professor of finance at Stanford Graduate School of Business and cofounder of Quantal International, a supplier of portfolio management systems, wrote in response to critics of the MPT paradigm,

> One of MPT's key insights is that while investors need to be compensated to bear risk, not all risks are rewarded. The market does not reward risks that can be "diversified away" by holding a bundle of investments, instead of a single investment. By recognizing that not all risks are rewarded, MPT helped establish the idea that a diversified portfolio can help investors earn a higher return for the same amount of risk. (p. 1 of electronic version)

Professor Pfleiderer acknowledged that in times of crisis, increased correlations reduce the benefit of diversification. He attributed this phenomenon to the (probably) increased importance of macro factors during a crisis. He maintained, however, that "the increased correlations limit, but do not eliminate, diversification's value" (p. 2 of electronic version).

Steven Greiner, director of portfolio risk at FactSet Research Systems, observed,

> The reason some believe diversification didn't work during the credit crisis of 2008 was that they didn't understand that *only* idiosyncratic risk is diversifiable. If 95% of your portfolio risk is systematic, whether you own 30 or 300 securities, when the system goes down, you're going down with it.

Dr. Greiner then pointed to a hypothetical portfolio that is not diversified across asset classes or factors. He concluded, "Active weighting is a very poor way to measure exposures and to achieve diversification."

This discussion is part of the debate on the interplay between dynamic asset allocation and diversification. On the one hand, diversification is a "static" concept: Defenders of diversification argue that by investing in a broad diversified portfolio, an investor is protected. Dynamic asset allocation, on the other hand, espouses the view that both correlations and expected returns change dynamically. Therefore, investors should adapt their diversification strategies to different market conditions.

Charles Chang, associate professor and director of the Master of Finance program at the Shanghai Advanced Institute of Finance, Shanghai Jiaotong University, commented:

> There has been a lot of discourse in recent years regarding (1) that cross-asset diversification is critical and (2) that given the demonstrated difficulty of generating alpha using stock/bond picking, asset allocation may be the key to a strong risk-adjusted return. That is, how much you decide to invest in equity versus real estate versus bonds, technology versus industrials, is the key to investment success. Indeed, some research has shown that the stocks picked are generally immaterial compared with the decision to overweight or underweight stocks in general. Similarly, funds of funds, in particular, focus their attention on being in the right industries at the right times rather than focusing on which stocks each money manager has chosen. The proliferation of ETFs [exchange-traded funds] has made this ever easier and more accessible to individual investors so it is probably time to place some focus on this discussion.

A dynamic approach to asset allocation has also been advocated from the point of view of the profile of the investor. Alan Brown (2013), senior adviser at Schroders Investment Management, advocates a dynamic approach to asset allocation that naturally takes into account a fund's individual characteristics, its regulatory environment, and its risk preferences. He commented, "It is increasingly widely recognized that the industry's best practice model of the last three decades has not served us well and is arguably not fit for [its] purpose[s]" (p. 1).

Critics argue that the increase of correlations in times of crisis is a structural phenomenon. Some thus conclude that diversification does not work when it is most needed. Thomas Kieselstein, CIO and managing partner at Quoniam, a quantitative asset management firm based in Frankfurt, remarked,

> The financial crisis has clearly shown that when you need diversification most, it may not work. Historical correlations may simply be wrong. Different liquidity of different asset classes may mean that some less risky assets may still be punished because they are tradable. We need better management of such extreme situations.

Changes in correlations may result from shifts in economic regimes. Dr. Lefeuvre (2012) wrote,

> Unconditional covariance is a myth: Regime dependence has to be understood. Asset returns still depend on macro factors, but within specific regimes. Economists have to identify regimes (Where are we? Where could

we be?) and then model returns within regimes. It can be even more complicated as previously identified regimes may entice different returns behavior in the future (ex: inflation regimes). (p. 17)

In addition to the problem related to the time-varying nature of correlations, there are estimation issues. Critics argue that diversification is a mathematical concept that is theoretically valid but whose applicability is difficult. Diversification requires the estimation—more precisely, the forecasting—of the covariance matrix of returns. The estimation of covariance matrices is, however, subject to many uncertainties. In large portfolios, in particular, empirical covariance matrices are very noisy because of the large number of entries.

Ormerod and Helbing (2012) considered studies by econophysicists who used random matrix theory.[13] They noted that these studies showed that "correlation matrices determined from financial return series contain such a high amount of noise that . . . 94% of [their] spectrum could be fitted by that of a purely random matrix" (p. 151).

These critiques are not new. Jacques Olivier, professor of finance and program director of the Master in Finance at HEC, Paris, cited work by Olivier Ledoit and Michael Wolf (2003) on estimating risk of the variance–covariance matrix and the implications for efficient portfolios and a paper by François Longin and Bruno Solnik (1995) on the behavior of correlations during extreme events.

Even more fundamental critiques of diversification have been made. One such critique comes from ETH Zurich's Professor Didier Sornette. He believes that the concept of diversification is intrinsically inapplicable to financial markets because of their nonstationary nature.

Michael Dever, CEO and director of research at Brandywine Asset Management, and John Uebler (2012) critiqued diversification and related buy-and-hold investment strategies from another point of view. They wrote,

> [C]onventional wisdom [i.e., diversification] is flawed because it is dependent on a single set of "return drivers". . . . The fact is that when large portfolios of stocks are bought "for the long run," diversification does not protect and capital destruction is virtually guaranteed. (p. 1 of electronic version)

Dever and Uebler suggested that proper portfolio diversification should be based on the distribution of *risk* across numerous return drivers. They defined a "return driver" as the primary underlying condition propelling the price of a market. They asked,

> So, is there an alternative approach to diversification which does not rely on these flawed assumptions of conventional investment wisdom? . . . The

---

[13]See Laloux, Cizeau, Bouchaud, and Potters (2000) and Plerou, Gobikrishnan, Rosenow, Amaral, and Stanley (1999).

answer is [that] proper portfolio diversification is based on the distribution of risk across numerous "return drivers." (p 1 of electronic version)

Andrew Ang, professor of business at Columbia Business School, also believes that returns result from drivers, but he identifies a different set of return drivers. In his forthcoming book, *Asset Management*, Professor Ang suggests that one set of factors describes fundamental, economy-wide variables, like growth, inflation, volatility, productivity, and demographic risk while another set consists of tradable investment styles like the market portfolio, value–growth investing, and momentum investing. The economic theory behind factors can be either rational, where the factors have high returns over the long run to compensate for their low returns during bad times, or behavioral, where the factor risk premiums result from the nonrational behavior of agents that is not arbitraged away.

In summary, although diversification is considered to be a sound probabilistic concept, the benefits of diversification may change as market states change or, in particular, as correlations and expected returns change. The naive belief that by simply diversifying a portfolio the investor is protected against major losses is just that—naive. Large losses in well-diversified portfolios may occur because of excessive leverage, the fat-tailedness of returns, or simply because the returns of most assets and asset classes are negative in a market downturn.

Two of the authors of this book, Frank Fabozzi and Sergio Focardi, made this point in the *Journal of Portfolio Management* in their editorial titled "Diversification: Should We Be Diversifying Trends?" (2010). Fabozzi and Focardi argued that the increase in correlations of returns is not the critical phenomenon that characterizes market crises. The real problem, they wrote, is the *inversion of trends*. In time of crisis, most stock returns become negative and the benefit of diversification is reduced. Using standard statistical tests, Fabozzi and Focardi showed that the behavior of indices such as the S&P 500 in the past 20 years does not follow a random walk but, rather, is characterized by the reversal of local trends. An upward/downward trend can be characterized by a regime of positive/negative returns; a trend reversal can be characterized as a regime shift. The authors argued that a different concept of diversification should be introduced: diversification of local trends. They suggested that investors concentrate on asset classes or market sectors that are characterized by local trends that are not correlated. To make diversification beneficial, they argued, investors should look at trend reversals and at correlations between local trends.

Some might argue that the proof of the existence of different "states" or local trends rests on subtle statistical tests and is, therefore, not solid. The authors believe, however, that this criticism is ill conceived: The statistical test on the existence of trends is one of many empirical proofs that economies and financial markets are essentially unstable and are, more frequently than not, in conditions of nonequilibrium. States represent the buildup of internal market tensions and their subsequent release.

Ultimately, the debate about diversification rests on whether changes in correlations and expected returns are random and unpredictable or whether they are the result of partially predictable changes in market states. Predictability of these parameters would lead to a shift away from naive diversification and into dynamic asset allocation.

Jaap van Dam, head of strategy and research at the Dutch healthcare workers' pension fund PGGM, commented,

> I personally and the whole Dutch fund management industry subscribe to the big lessons of modern portfolio theory, but there are a number of things that should be considered going forward. There is the need for lots of new thinking. Typical MPT and diversification has been to diversify by adding more and more countries, more and more assets. But this is not satisfying. It is necessary to consider factors, time diversification. For example, in theory, diversification is measured along the lines of standard deviation, a market index. But one needs an understanding of what one is investing in and the possibility to influence the firms one invests in. Regime shifts should also play a role in thinking about portfolio construction. What is key is to make sure that on the longer horizon, one fulfills the objective of the fund (i.e., the investor) and does so successfully under all circumstances.

We will look at the implications of this discussion on teaching diversification in the following chapters.

Optimization: Diversification Formalized

In the methodology of neoclassical finance, "efficient diversification of portfolios" (Markowitz's phrase) is accomplished through mean–variance optimization (MVO). Broadly, *optimization* refers to a family of approaches to portfolio construction that are grounded in Markowitz's work but that may differ from his original formulation to deal with the model's unrealistic assumptions and the practical challenges in implementation. The differences include the use of alternative risk measures, such as tracking error and value at risk, consideration of transaction costs, portfolio management constraints, and sensitivity to the estimates of expected returns and covariances. In addition, new trends and developments in MVO include risk-parity portfolios, the mixing of sources of alpha, and practical multiperiod portfolio optimization (for a discussion of these extensions and trends, see Kolm, Tütüncu, and Fabozzi 2014).

Some observers, particularly in the industry and in the popular press, refer to optimization and related techniques as MPT. This nomenclature is confusing: Optimization is not "modern," nor is it a "theory." It is a tool. For a given set of inputs, the output portfolio is efficient according to a set of prespecified criteria. Some utility theory lies behind this claim, but it is not a theory in a philosophical sense (i.e., it is not empirically verifiable or falsifiable).

The term "MPT" is also used more broadly to refer to the entire body of quantitative finance knowledge developed between Markowitz (1952) and, to give one person's view of the end point, the option-pricing work of Fischer Black and Myron Scholes (1973) or dynamic portfolio optimization (Merton 1973).

For Markowitz's original method, we use the term MVO. MVO requires knowledge of expected returns and the covariance matrix of returns. Several variations on MVO have been proposed. They are based on utility functions and might require the knowledge of the joint distribution of returns.

Following the 2007–09 financial crisis, MVO was declared by some to be "dead," together with the entire body of quantitative finance knowledge captured by use of the broader term MPT. The critique focused on the fact that a true risk–return trade-off went amiss. Most assets had negative returns, and forecasting tools had failed. Three aspects of the issue can be distinguished:

- the validity of MVO as a decision-making rule,

- the applicability of MVO in light of analysts' ability to forecast, and

- the applicability of MVO in a period of negative returns—that is, large negative market swings.

The critique and defense of MVO are summarized in **Exhibit 2.2**.

As with diversification, the mathematics of MVO is not at issue. The question is: Does the math of MVO correspond to the empirical reality of investments? The problem is whether or not a meaningful separation can be empirically found between diversifiable, unrewarded risk and nondiversifiable, rewarded risk. The defenders of MVO maintain that this separation can be found.

Some argue that, although neoclassical finance as it is presently practiced is not a realistic framework for investment decision making, incremental

Exhibit 2.2. The Defense and Critique of MVO

Defense of MVO	Critique of MVO
MVO is a fundamental building block of investment theory and practice because (1) it prescribes the optimization of a risk–return trade-off and (2) it prescribes that we look at the global risk of a portfolio, not only the risk of its individual components. Incremental improvement in the method is possible, but the fundamental concept is sound. Liabilities may be incorporated as "assets held short."	MVO is an oversimplification that relies on diversification in a naive way: It does not recognize the difficulty in forecasting expected returns and covariances—or forecasting the multivariate probability distribution of returns. As a decision-making rule, MVO does not explicitly recognize the liability aspects of investment management, so elaborate work-arounds are required. Also, basic MVO does not consider fat tails.

changes are possible. FactSet's Dr. Greiner stressed the *nonnormality* of the distribution of returns. He commented,

> MPT is 1960s technology and thought, not current thought. It is outdated in the sense that it is completely linear and Gaussian theory. Covariance is linear. Mean–variance optimization focuses on maximizing error estimation. Fat tails are real. What people should be focusing on is how to reduce estimation error, how to account for fat-tail correlations and extreme-event stress testing.

Another constructive critique of MVO and its associated portfolio prescriptions came from Bruce Jacobs, principal of Jacobs Levy Equity Management and author of *Capital Ideas and Market Realities* (1999). He said,

> Financial markets have changed considerably since Harry Markowitz introduced MPT in 1952. In particular, leverage is a lot more prominent as a result of the growth of futures and options, structured finance products, hedge funds, and short selling. MPT, as implemented through mean–variance optimization, recognizes portfolio leverage only to the extent that leverage increases portfolio volatility. It is silent on other, substantial risks that are unique to using leverage, including the possibility of margin calls, which can force borrowers to liquidate securities at adverse prices; potential losses exceeding the capital invested; and even bankruptcy.

The recent literature on liquidity and financial frictions addresses this issue to some extent (see, e.g., Adler 2012).

Dr. Jacobs cited articles co-authored with Jacobs Levy Equity Management cofounder Kenneth Levy on leverage aversion and portfolio optimality (2012) and on leverage aversion, efficient frontiers, and the efficient region (2013). In a 2014 article, Jacobs and Levy argue that traditional optimization is not optimal for leverage-averse investors because it provides no guidance on how to identify the optimal level of leverage. Dr. Jacobs believes that an alternative approach that they propose—the mean–variance-leverage optimization model, which balances a portfolio's expected return against both volatility risk and leverage risk—allows for determination of the optimal portfolio for an investor with a given aversion to the unique risks of leverage.

Some propose incremental changes based on concepts of liquidity. As discussed in the previous chapter, Michael Oliver, senior lecturer in finance at the Open University and cofounder and director of the investment firm Global Partnership of Family Offices, believes that neoclassical finance is an incomplete theory that needs to take into consideration "the supply and demand for money and credit, and other flows of funds that influence the level of asset prices as a whole" (Pepper and Oliver 2006, p. 5).

Others suggest that the doubts that have been cast on neoclassical finance are huge because of the narrow notion of risk on which it is based. Quoniam's

Mr. Kieselstein, for one, believes that the notion of risk must be amplified. He commented,

> Risk goes much further than the standard deviation of historical returns. Effects like the minimum-volatility anomaly as well as the earlier style premia (value, size, momentum) clearly demonstrate that.

Still others opine that MVO is of little use at all because it addresses only "benign" risks—namely, expected fluctuations in asset values as measured by standard deviation. ETH Zurich's Professor Sornette remarked, "Markowitz and Sharpe are blind to systemic risks and thus blind to the kind of huge losses of a systemic character [that can occur]." We discuss the issue of crises in the last section of this chapter.

A distinction should be made between MVO as a decision-making rule and our ability to forecast. Sébastien Lleo, professor of finance at NEOMA Business School, remarked that Markowitz's seminal 1952 article describes a two-stage portfolio selection process. The objective of MVO was to provide an efficient tool for Step 2 of the process. Step 1 is the formation of relevant beliefs about the future performance of each asset in the opportunity set, including the correlations of assets. MVO then makes Step 2, the choice of the portfolio to be held, a matter of mechanics. Professor Lleo remarked, "Markowitz does not say anything about how to formulate these 'beliefs,' how to generate forecasts, or about the actual occurrence of events. He does not say what markets can or cannot do." Professor Lleo views MVO as a set of prescriptions that we might find more or less adapted to our needs but argues that the critical task is *making the forecasts* that the set of prescriptions requires.

This last comment summarizes the position of MVO. In itself, MVO is a mathematical method that can be extended to cover a broad set of decision-making procedures. But its use has two limitations:

- First, the forecasts: There are empirical questions that cannot be solved theoretically—in particular, our ability to make forecasts, primarily of expected returns but also of covariances, and the real benefit from optimization and diversification.

- Second, the applicability of MVO as a decision-making framework: Although quite flexible, MVO does not naturally encompass important instances, such as asset and liability management. These concerns can be addressed through complex work-arounds that have become widely used in practice (see, e.g., Sharpe and Tint 1990).

Dutch pension fund PGGM's Jaap van Dam commented,

> In asset allocation, we need to understand the limitations of the traditional mean–variance approach: It is just a tool that transforms mechanically our

assumptions to asset weights. Understanding the limitations and possible errors of the assumptions is central.

Our limited ability to make forecasts has led some to suggest that we abandon altogether the notion of optimality. James Montier (2012), a member of fund manager GMO's asset allocation team, argued,

> I don't believe that optimal can exist in an *ex ante* sense without the aid of a crystal ball. Of course, *ex post*, it is trivial to construct an optimal portfolio. However, since I've yet to encounter an investor armed with a fully functioning crystal ball, I would suggest that we need to abandon the pursuit of the optimal and instead aim for robustness. *Ex ante* optimality is inherently fragile: It is only optimal for your best guess of the future. (p. 11)

We look at the implications of these critiques for the teaching of MVO and related aspects of MPT in later chapters.

Capital Asset Pricing Model

The CAPM is an asset-pricing theory based on the assumption that all investors share the same rational expectations and apply modern portfolio theory in its mean–variance implementation. The key quantitative finding of the CAPM is that the expected excess return of each asset is proportional to the expected excess return of the market. The proportionality factor is the covariance between the returns of each asset and market returns.

CAPM is a general-equilibrium asset-pricing theory. It implies the *fund separation theorem*, which states that all investors hold the same risky portfolio, namely, the market portfolio. In practice, however, the CAPM is often confused with a one-factor model. The framework for our discussion of the defense of CAPM theory and practice and the critique is summarized in **Exhibit 2.3**.

Exhibit 2.3.   The Defense and Critique of CAPM Theory and Practice

Defense of CAPM Theory	Defense of CAPM Practice	Critique of CAPM Theory and Practice
Defenders of the CAPM as a theory argue that the basic intuition of the CAPM is still valid and pertinent—that is, nondiversifiable risk is rewarded and diversifiable risk is unrewarded.	Defenders of the CAPM as a single-factor model hold that it is a good approximation to asset pricing and that no obviously better model exists. They argue that deviations from the CAPM are only local random fluctuations.	Critics observe that the CAPM, as any other general equilibrium theory, is based on unrealistic assumptions. Empirically, the CAPM does not capture the most fundamental aspects of risk (i.e., systemic risk) nor does it capture the multiplicity of factors and market states. Critics also cite a myriad of studies showing that the CAPM does not produce exact or even good return forecasts.

Let's start with the defenders. Many view the poor performance of the CAPM during the 2007–09 financial crisis as an expression of normal statistical fluctuations. Mr. Waring remarked,

> CAPM provides statistical forecasts of distributions of returns, not exact forecasts. When a model does not seem to work over a particular period, people often say that the model is invalid. But it needs to be pointed out that it is the *random* part of the model that they are seeing; it does not mean the model is not working. Consider a typical pension fund, consisting of 60% equities and 40% bonds, which has a return distribution with a standard deviation of 10% around a mean of 8% as forecast by the CAPM: There's lots of room for disappointment from that random standard deviation component without concluding that the model didn't work.

In other words, the CAPM is a statistical model, and for it to perform poorly in some periods is normal, especially because the standard deviation of returns is often larger than their expected return value. This point of view upholds the theory that financial markets are stable, self-correcting structures that fluctuate around situations of equilibrium; large losses in periods of crisis do not invalidate models such as the CAPM. The stochastic nature of the model does not rule out large market movements.

This approach opens an epistemological problem. If we believe that losses of the order of 50% of the global market value are normal events that can be neither foreseen nor prevented, what type of finance theory do we have? What do we know except that the markets operate with extreme uncertainty?

Other defenders argue that the CAPM is an important theoretical framework that sheds light on the process of price formation, despite the fact that the model's forecasts have been found inaccurate by empirical tests. Professor Ang believes that the CAPM was revolutionary because it was the first cogent theory to recognize that the risk of an asset was not how that asset behaved in isolation, but how that asset moved in relation to other assets and to the market as a whole. He argues that, although a spectacular empirical failure, the CAPM is, conceptually, an important theory: It predicts that asset risk premiums depend only on the asset's beta and there is only one factor that matters, the market portfolio. While these predictions have been demolished in numerous empirical studies, Professor Ang believes that the basic intuition of the CAPM still holds true—that is, that the factors underlying the assets determine asset risk premiums and that these risk premiums are compensation for investors weathering losses during bad times.

Jim Liew, assistant professor of finance at the Johns Hopkins Carey Business School, noted that one should understand the limits of the CAPM and its subsequent development. Commenting on the theory of finance and the CAPM, he said,

> It is important to understand the foundations of finance theory, to build upon it, and to know its limitations. Blindly following CAPM is dangerous. CAPM gives us a rich theory, but it can completely break down, especially when markets become distressed.

On the application side, some observed that what is used in practice is not the CAPM but a one-factor model. Professor Lleo noted that the CAPM is a theory that is often confused with factor models. He argues that the two should be kept distinct:

> Sharpe follows in Markowitz's footsteps. His greatest contributions are the factor models, which provide an efficient implementation of Markowitz's idea, and the CAPM. Although the CAPM is taught in every corporate finance, portfolio management, and stock valuation class, what most practitioners use on a daily basis is a model half-way between the factor model and the CAPM. This reveals a deeply rooted ambiguity at the heart of finance: What economic theoreticians see as crucial is often very different from what corporate executives or financial market participants judge useful. Yet, we often use the same language to refer to the abstract result (the CAPM) and to its pragmatic sibling (the single-factor model).

Practitioners who consider that the CAPM is, in practice, a one-factor model, observed that a one-factor model is a poor approximation of reality. Ever since factor models were proposed by Stephen Ross in 1976, the debate on the number and type of factors needed to describe returns has a long history. But there are theoretical problems associated with factor models. For example, when performing factor analysis of empirical return series, no reasonably small number of factors produces uncorrelated residuals (the desired result). If residuals are allowed to be correlated, however, we may be able to identify factors in residuals. A clear distinction can be made between global factors and the factors of the residuals only in the limiting case of infinite markets (by which we mean idealized conceptual markets formed by an infinite number of stocks). In finite markets, factors cannot be uniquely identified, which justifies the proliferation of commercially available factor models.

Schroders' Alan Brown remarked,

> Everyone needs to realize that CAPM is a partial equilibrium model. It is an abstraction of reality; it assumes equilibrium and normal distributions. But a one-factor beta model cannot capture reality. It is important, but it does not correctly characterize markets. Take, for example, a cap-weighted benchmark. There are vastly more left- or right-tailed events than those

assumed in CAPM. There are persistent anomalies. Fama and French's [1992, 1993] three-factor model, which adds value and size, is a good step forward, but it is still just an abstraction of reality.

In summary, despite all the critiques—CAPM is a flawed partial equilibrium theory and the one-factor model, sloppy econometrics—and the fact that the forecasts given by the CAPM have been found wanting in numerous empirical studies, the CAPM is still widely considered (at least in academia) to be a valid theoretical framework for asset pricing. In practice, the one-factor model is considered to be little more than a first approximation; a richer factor structure is called for.

We look at the implications of these ideas and findings on teaching the CAPM in later chapters.

The Efficient Market Hypothesis

The efficient market hypothesis (EMH) was first introduced by Eugene Fama, professor of finance at the University of Chicago Booth School of Business, in the 1960s and has since become one of central concepts in mainstream finance. Actually, the EMH is made of two distinct hypotheses:

- Asset prices have theoretical values, their "fair" prices.

- Market prices coincide with theoretical prices.

From these two parts of the EMH, one can easily understand why it led to the (now widespread) practice of investing in broad indices. Twenty-five years ago, Michael Jensen (1978), Harvard University emeritus professor, wrote, "I believe there is no other proposition in economics which has more solid empirical evidence supporting it than the Efficient Market Hypothesis" (p. 95).

Nevertheless, the EMH is the concept that raised perhaps the most debate after recent market crises. Here is why: An academic hypothesis that states that markets are "efficient" (insofar as market prices are always equal to theoretical prices) seems to be at odds with the reality of a market that lost 57% of its value from the market peak in October 2007 to its bottom in March 2009 and then bounced back to its precrash high within four years. How can all these different prices for the "same asset" be "right"? Consider this remark from PGGM's Jaap van Dam: "In general, what bothers me when I look at the past 30 years is that markets were supposed to be efficient but in the end, the investment managers are price takers, not price setters."

Professor Jensen's view remained the prevailing view for more than 30 years, but many dissenting opinions can be cited. Robert Shiller, professor of economics at Yale University, tested the EMH by comparing the (high) volatility of market prices to the (low) volatility of dividends and reached the conclusion that fluctuations of market prices are inconsistent with the EMH. After the market crash of 1987, Professor Shiller (2010b) referred to the efficient market hypothesis as "the most remarkable error in the history of economic theory."

In an interview with *NY Times* journalist Joe Nocera (2009), Jeremy Grantham, cofounder of and market strategist at GMO, added his critique:

> The incredibly inaccurate efficient market theory was believed in totality by many of our financial leaders, and believed in part by almost all. It left our economic and government establishment sitting by confidently, even as a lethally dangerous combination of asset bubbles, lax controls, pernicious incentives, and wickedly complicated instruments led to our current plight. (p. 2 of electronic document)

Why do so many economists and financial economists continue to subscribe to the EMH? As with many other concepts and principles of prevailing finance theory, the theoretical foundation of EMH appears strong, so strong that the EMH is taken to be a self-evident proposition: Any deviation from true prices is perceived by speculators who immediately try to make a profit exploiting these deviations and, in so doing, realign prices to their true value.

This reasoning has been repeated over and over again in papers, books, lectures, and conferences. Despite the reasoning's apparent strength, however, it contains three questionable points:

1. What is the *theoretical* price of a financial asset?

2. How do we know it?

3. Do we have any reason to believe that the market value will move toward this hypothetical theoretical value?

Let's now examine the various points of view concerning the EMH. First, **Exhibit 2.4** summarizes views from the industry and academia.

Exhibit 2.4. The Defense and Critique of the EMH

Defense of the EMH	Empirical Critique of the EMH	Radical Critique of the EMH
The EMH is a sound concept and an empirically viable proposition. Speculators immediately spot any mispricing and realign market prices to their "true" theoretical value. Excess returns earned by forecasting markets are marginal and highly volatile. In practice, active portfolio managers have a devilishly hard time beating market benchmarks, which supports the EMH.	The EMH is conceptually sound but empirically false. Many tests show that market prices deviate from their theoretical values and that markets are subject to forecastable distortions.	The EMH is meaningless because the notion of the true price of an asset based on the present value of an infinite stream of cash flows is empirically meaningless. We need to consider forecastability, which is not equivalent to efficiency.

Robert Lucas, professor of economics at the University of Chicago, defended the EMH in his article "In Defense of the Dismal Science" (2009). It was written in response to a series of articles critical of mainstream macroeconomics that started with the *Economist*'s 16 July 2009 article "What Went Wrong with Economics and How the Discipline Should Change to Avoid the Mistakes of the Past." Professor Lucas argued that the theory propounded in the EMH has been thoroughly challenged and the accuracy of the hypothesis confirmed. He wrote,

> Over the years exceptions and "anomalies" have been discovered (even tiny departures are interesting if you are managing enough money) but for the purpose of macroeconomic analysis and forecasting these departures are too small to matter. (p. 1 of electronic document)

For Professor Lucas, the inability to predict events such as the failure of Lehman Brothers was a confirmation of the theory of market efficiency, one of whose main implications is that the price of a financial asset reflects all relevant information that is generally available. In defense of the EMH, he argued, "If an economist had a formula that could reliably forecast crises a week in advance, say, then that formula would become part of generally available information and prices would fall a week earlier" (p. 1 of electronic document).

Here Professor Lucas was equating "forecasts" with exact, deterministic forecasts. Indeed, we do not have this type of deterministic knowledge, but forecasts can be probabilistic—in the sense that analysts could recognize regime changes or when the economy is in a state of disequilibrium. If economists were able to give early warning of the increasing probability of an impending large market swing, this information would be helpful, and not only to asset managers. Consider the field of medicine, where preventive tests, although not exact, are useful because they give an early warning of the possible development of a given disease. Natixis's Dr. Lefeuvre (2012) wrote,

> Economists' job is not to tell you where the S&P 500 or the 10-year Treasury yields will be at year-end, but to send enough reliable signals on the regime switches or market-strained periods that take place between now and then. (p. 17)

Some argue that, although the EMH provides a useful conceptual framework, its importance should not be overstated. In other words, as useful as the EMH might be when considered a framework for thinking about markets, it should not be taken as an absolute theoretical principle. Financial assets are claims to future cash flows; hence, their value is somehow linked to a reference value. A reasonable assumption is that investors do not want to buy or sell assets priced too far from the reference value.

Professor Logue noted that, although a multitude of deviations from efficient behavior have been observed, most economists still hold to the EMH.

He remarked, "If you pick up a major textbook by, for example, Sharpe, you read that stocks are priced correctly. But there are actually massive anomalies in the micro and macro sense." Professor Logue questioned whether we have a viable asset-pricing theory:

> Do we have an asset-pricing theory? We sort of know what the model looks like. In bonds, we use the present value, coupons, parameters. For example, using the current rate on 10-year bonds we can calculate a good price. In stocks, we use the dividend growth model, the current dividend; the only question is the discount rate. But how well can we estimate? On foreign exchange, we don't know the model, the parameters. We have the McDonald hamburger index. There should be no difference in prices across countries, save for taxes, labor costs, and raw material costs. Nonetheless, there are often massive, inexplicable price discrepancies. The law of one price is supposed to prevail but often doesn't. Markets often behave in ways that cannot be explained by extant theory.

Regarding the law of one price, Professor Logue cited the trading rules that a group of New York City stockbrokers established among themselves in 1792.[14] Their objective was to ensure the same price for the same stock in simultaneous transactions. However, Professor Logue noted that with today's various trading venues, "dark pools," and algorithmic trading, if you and I wished to buy stock in Company X at the same time, we might pay different prices because of trading in different venues. He commented, "Market participants worry about this, but academics do not." Professor Logue cited Robert Shiller's work on irrational markets. Shiller (1981) observed that the present value of subsequent detrended real dividends is found to be a very stable and smooth series when compared with the actual detrended real stock price series. An efficient markets model that makes price the optimal forecast of the *ex post* rational price is inconsistent with these data.

Among those who poke holes in the efficient market hypothesis is Dr. Oliver, who argued that the EMH, like the rest of neoclassical finance, is an incomplete theory that needs to take *money* into consideration. He suggests that the best evaluation criteria for predicting future equity market returns are liquidity and psychology (that is, human behavior).

The role of credit and debt creation in forming asset market prices and bubbles is central to the theories developed by ETH Zurich's Professor Didier Sornette. Professor Sornette observed that financial markets are essentially nonstationary and unstable. He attributes market instability, which

---

[14]In 1792, 24 stockbrokers in New York City signed what is referred to as the Buttonwood Agreement (so named because it was signed under a buttonwood tree on Wall Street). The agreement fixed trading rules on the exchange that was to become the New York Stock Exchange.

contradicts market efficiency, to the process of excessive credit and debt creation, similar to the thinking of the late Hyman Minsky's (1992) critique.[15]

Sornette argued in "The Illusion of the Perpetual Money Machine" (Sornette and Cauwels 2012) that financial bubbles and the ensuing crises are ultimately phenomena of asset inflation because of excessive generation of credit and debt that stays in the financial sector, thereby rendering the sector fragile. To provide a simple intuition of the process, the authors used a sequence of graphics that first showed the behavior of the S&P 500 with respect to US gross domestic product and then showed the parallel behavior of wages, savings, corporate profits, and debt. The impact of money generation on the economy and financial markets becomes quite clear from these graphics.

Commenting on the market's recovery after the recent financial crisis, Professor Sornette remarked,

> The markets have bounced back due to the QEs [quantitative easings]. This is an artificial pumping up of financial markets that has no solid fundamental foundation. It is an illusion that a savvy investor should be aware of and take corresponding precautionary measures.

Clearly, Sornette and Cauwel's theory runs against the EMH: A market where asset prices rise primarily because of demand artificially created by the excessive generation of credit and debt cannot be considered an efficient market. If we accept that money generation is (at least partially) responsible for the price level of financial assets, we must conclude that there is no single, theoretically correct price. The same asset can have two "correct" prices in two different monetary conditions. Asset inflation is a deviation from rationality more fundamental than any cognitive bias of investors.

Other analysts also ascribe money or liquidity an essential role in the pricing of assets. Brandywine Asset Management's Michael Dever remarked that the apparent intrinsic return from investing in US stocks over the past 100+ years was the result of two primary return drivers: (1) the aggregate profit (or earnings) growth of the companies that constitute the "market" and (2) the multiple that people were willing to pay for those earnings (i.e., the price-to-earnings ratio, or P/E). Dever and Uebler (2012) argued that the P/E is the result of the level of demand, which is determined by psychological factors. Analyzing the S&P 500 Total Return (TR) Index, the authors observed,

> In any period of less than 10 years, earnings accounted for less than 25% of the price change in the S&P 500 TR index, while changes in the P/E ratio accounted for more than 75% of this price change. (p. 2)

---

[15]Minsky proposed his financial instability hypothesis (FIH) in a 1992 working paper. According to Minsky, capitalist economies exhibit inflations and debt deflations that—because of the fragile financial systems—can end in financial and economic crises. Minsky positioned his FIH as an interpretation of Keynes's General Theory.

Paul Woolley, who cofounded GMO Woolley, the London affiliate of the Boston-based fund management firm GMO, and served as its managing director, suggests that there is yet another explanation for why markets are not efficient. In his paper "Why Are Financial Markets So Inefficient and Exploitative—and a Suggested Remedy," Dr. Woolley (2010) argues that the source of market inefficiency is the principal–agent problem. He wrote, "Agents have better information and different objectives than their customers (principals) and this asymmetry is . . . the source of inefficiency—mispricing, bubbles, and crashes" (p. 121). Dr. Woolley subsequently founded the Paul Woolley Centre for the Study of Capital Markets Dysfunctionality at the London School of Economics.[16]

Why such a divergence of opinions about a concept—the efficient market hypothesis—that should be fundamental? Economists Bernard Guerrien and Ozgur Gun (2011) offered an answer in their article in the online *Real-World Economics Review*. Guerrien and Gun critiqued Fama's famous statement of the EMH, which has become *the* statement of the EMH: "A market in which prices at any time 'fully reflect' available information is called 'efficient.'" They observed that Fama himself was careful in his 1970 paper to avoid using this sentence as a definition of the EMH. The words "fully reflect" appear in quotation marks; Fama understood that this definition of the EMH was not tenable and quickly moved on to alternative definitions of market efficiency based either on equilibrium models or on the (near) impossibility of beating the market.

What the proponents of the EMH want to argue is that (1) given all current generally available information, we can determine the theoretical price of an asset and (2) a market is efficient if observed prices are equal to or close to the theoretical values. Otherwise, the market is inefficient. An implicit addition to this statement is as follows: Markets tend to be efficient; if markets show inefficiencies, these inefficiencies tend to disappear as markets revert to their theoretical value thanks to the action of market participants.

The link between the EMH and asset pricing is provided by the notion that the theoretical value of an asset is the present value of its future discounted cash flows: Markets are efficient if the price of each asset equals or comes close to the present value of its future discounted cash flows. This notion replaced the idea that markets are efficient if prices "fully reflect" current available information. This change did not, however, add clarity because the present value of future discounted cash flows cannot be empirically ascertained. Guerrien and Gun (2011) remarked that the EMH is an empty concept because cash flows cannot be forecasted into the distant future. In short, the twin hypotheses of asset pricing and the EMH are not verifiable. As

---

[16]For information on the Paul Woolley Centre, see http://business.uts.edu.au/qfrc/pwc/.

mentioned previously, Joseph McCauley (2009), University of Houston professor of physics, observed that the concept of an infinite stream of cash flows is a purely abstract mathematical concept that is not observable. As such, the concept of an infinite stream of cash flows should not be part of any empirical theory.

In this regard, the difference between the conceptual approach used in finance theory and that used in the physical sciences should not be overlooked. In the physical sciences, one studies "reality as it is." Scientific models aim at representing reality, typically for forecasting purposes—for example, to determine how an airplane's wing design will perform in flight. Scientists do not make statements about the difference between actual observations and what the observations *should* be. Any such attempt would be considered unscientific—and potentially quite dangerous!

In economic and finance theory, financial markets and economies at large are considered to be intelligent processors of information but prone to make mistakes and subject to biases. Hence, we have the distinction between a real price and a theoretical price. This distinction carries a strong ideological appeal: Markets where real prices are equal to theoretical prices would be "efficient," capable of receiving and processing information without distortions.

The question is how to define the theoretical price. Fama and some other proponents of the EMH have understood the difficulty and redefined the EMH in terms of one of its consequences: lack of predictability. If markets are efficient, prices are what they should be. Hence, prices move only in response to information not yet known and not forecastable. As a consequence, returns are not forecastable. If returns are not forecastable, no excess return can be earned by trading. The EMH has thus come to be identified with the impossibility of systematically earning excess returns.

Alternatively, some proponents of the EMH have defined it in terms of asset-pricing models: Markets are efficient if current prices are equal to theoretical prices according to asset-pricing models. Fama himself said that testing the EMH is a double test of the EMH and of an asset-pricing model. This approach comes down to stating that if the test of the EMH fails, the cause can be either market inefficiencies or the fact that the asset-pricing model used does not give the true price of assets.

In summary, the critique of the efficient market hypothesis following the 2007–09 financial crisis has centered around the statement that the large market swings characterizing this and other financial crises are incompatible with the notion that markets are populated by rational agents who price assets rationally as a function of all generally available information.

The traditional defense of the EMH has been that large market swings can be seen as occasional fluctuations of an otherwise stable market. The EMH holds that market prices equal theoretical prices. Theoretical prices are defined in terms of future cash flows, but there is no agreement on how to forecast these cash flows. In other words, there is no agreement on the precise value of theoretical prices.

As mentioned, Fama himself understood this difficulty and proposed to identify market efficiency with market unpredictability. In addition, Burton Malkiel (2011), a "founding father" of the EMH and author of *A Random Walk Down Wall Street* (1973), stated that the EMH does not imply that asset prices are always correct but, rather, that they are always wrong! Moreover, he added, the EMH does not imply that bubbles in asset prices are impossible, only that arbitrage opportunities for riskless gains do not exist (i.e., there is no free lunch). These statements are, effectively, a redefinition of the EMH in terms of profit opportunities, a reinterpretation of why investors cannot beat the market.

Defining market efficiency in terms of market profitability is legitimate. Two co-authors of this book, Focardi and Fabozzi (2012), argued that market efficiency is a quantitative concept—essentially related to forecastability and realizable profitability—that takes into account the impact of a strategy on the market. This notion is very different, however, from the notion that market prices are always equal to theoretical prices. Stating that forecasting prices and making excess profits are difficult is not the same as stating that prices are correct.

We will look at the implications of these discussions for teaching the EMH in later chapters.

Risk Measurement and Management

Risk management has also come in for criticism since the recent financial crisis. The *concept* of risk management is not, however, in question. The questions relate to the adequacy of the *risk measurement methods and models* used and the *scope* of risk management. Quoniam's Thomas Kieselstein remarked,

> It can be argued that risk models were a major driver in the buildup of the financial crisis. Many of those sophisticated models completely miscalculated certain structural risks like, for example, the housing bubble. The need to rethink risk management strategies and risk models has become evident.

Exhibit 2.5 provides a summary of the critiques of measures of risk forecasting and the current definitions of risk.

Exhibit 2.5. Critiques of Risk Measures, Risk Forecasting, and the Definitions of Risk

Risk Measures	Risk Forecasting	Definitions of Risk
Critics claim present risk measures, such as value at risk, are oversimplified.	Critics blame crises on an insufficient understanding of the risk processes—in particular, the lack of our ability to forecast systemic risk.	Critics claim that present definitions of risk are too narrow. They blame the crisis on practitioners' focus on market-related risks, whereas risk includes credit risk, liquidity risk, systemic risk, operational risk, and (geo)political risk.

Mr. Waring commented on the danger of taking too simplistic a view of risk management:

> As regards risk management, the notion many people seem to have is that if you take more risk you will get a higher return. But that isn't what we teach. Rather, we teach that a higher expected return is associated with higher market risk. But what "higher market risk" means is a "higher standard deviation of returns." And greater risk thus means that there is a greater possibility of being strongly disappointed as the actual realized return is drawn from the urn of that larger standard deviation. It is too simple to think that more return is the natural consequence of more risk.

Moreover, just because someone is a long-term investor does not mean that it is safe for that person to take on more risk. The popular misconception is that risk goes away with time. It is not true. Risk to wealth actually *increases* proportionally to the square root of time. Even over very long periods, the expected return can be disappointing. People expecting an 8% return from the S&P 500, for example, for the 12 years starting with 2000 and going through 2011 earned just 0.05% a year on average. As a consequence, a dollar of initial investment that might have been worth well more than $2 if things had gone as expected was worth barely slightly more than a dollar—after 12 years.

As for inadequate risk measures, critics of current risk management practices observe that most asset management firms still use measures based on the assumption of normality, such as VaR. In a paper based on his speech delivered at the 65th CFA Institute Annual Conference in Chicago, fund manager GMO's James Montier (2012) remarked,

> Using VaR is like buying a car with an airbag that is guaranteed to fail just when you need it, or relying on body armour that you know keeps out 95% of the bullets. VaR cuts off the very part of the distribution of returns we should be worried about: the tails. (p. 3)

Some believe that concepts such as VaR, which is a confidence interval, are misunderstood. Schroders' Alan Brown noted that not only are widely used risk metrics inadequate, they are also "very badly understood." He said that a lot of confusion about VaR still exists:

> Many people take it to measure the maximum likely loss, but it actually measures the minimum loss. Even worse, *conditional VaR* is a weighted measure which assumes a normal distribution. In addition, widely used measures such as VaR assume that one acts alone while, in fact, we all use largely the same model. This creates systemic risk through contagion as many market participants end up doing the same thing at the same time—sell.

Professor Chang, of Shanghai Advanced Institute of Finance, observed that the financial crisis of 2007–2009, together with the earlier failure of the hedge fund Long-Term Capital Management, calls for a review of how we measure risk:

> [These events] require us to discuss a broader range of risk management measures, including going beyond normal distributions and discussing the importance of nonnormal evaluations, value-at-risk, and extreme events (so-called black swans). Some particular focus on potential loss functions and the left end of the distribution are particularly interesting. Indeed, a lot of literature and time, in the past, especially in investment texts, has been focused on equity markets and two-tailed risk. The fixed-income markets, we have seen, have led to the largest two collapses in the last decade or so. It is important, now, to understand credit risk evaluation and some of the ways we evaluate these issues. Collapse models are ever more important as are discussions of cross-market contagion.

As with most tasks related to investment management, however, the ability to forecast (quantitatively and qualitatively) and to determine future distributions of probability are the critical tasks. Can we really forecast the probability of large losses—the probability not only of major crises but of losses in general?

Defenders of mainstream economic and finance theory often hold that large market swings cannot be forecasted. In finance, losses, like any other major market event, cannot be *deterministically* forecasted. Forecasting is carried out in terms of *probability*. For example, we can assess whether we are in a state where a trend reversal is highly probable or not. As mentioned, Natixis CIO and chief economist for the Americas Evariste Lefeuvre argues that the economist's job is to send portfolio managers reliable signals on the likelihood of future regime switches or market-strained periods.

Professor Ang observed that an element of subjectivity is intrinsic in risk measurement. In his forthcoming book on asset management, he noted that while we think of risk today in terms of probability functions encompassing many different kinds of events, including that probabilities themselves change over time, risk in financial economics is inherently a subjective concept: The procedure used to estimate probabilities and the model that is behind the estimation impart subjectivity.

The language of risk measurement might be misleading. Today, risk is associated with *uncertainty*; in the original Markowitz framework, risk is equated to variance. A highly risky asset is an asset whose future return distribution has a large variance. Returns, therefore, are uncertain, and the risk–return trade-off is a trade-off between expectations and uncertainty. The notion of volatility is also based on the notion of uncertainty: Volatility is the magnitude of the error term, the residual uncertainty associated with modeling. A highly volatile market is a market where unpredictable fluctuations are large in comparison with expectations.

Both in the common language and in the current practice of risk management, however, risk is equated with the *probability that adverse events will occur* and/or the *magnitude of such events*. The distinction between risk as a high level of uncertainty and risk as a high probability of loss is particularly important for understanding the risk of large adverse market swings. A high risk of a crisis is a high probability that that there will be a large drop in market value; it is not increasing uncertainty about future returns. To appreciate the difference and the potential contradiction between the two concepts, suppose that at a certain moment we forecast a significant increase in the standard deviation of future returns—that is, an increase in *volatility*. This implies that we are more uncertain about the future; we anticipate the possibility of bad outcomes in terms of returns but also, perhaps, of big gains.

Hans Brachinger (2002), professor in the Department of Quantitative Economics at Switzerland's University of Fribourg, wrote that, despite the importance of risk, there is little consensus about its definition. He cited empirical studies in which typically two dimensions appear to determine perceived risk: the amount of potential loss and the probability of loss. Whatever measure we use, *probabilistic* forecasting is the critical task in measuring market risk. We say that returns can be forecast in a probabilistic sense if the conditional distribution of returns at time t changes as a function of information available at time t. We can further distinguish whether the expectation of returns changes or whether only the shape—that is, higher moments—of the distribution of returns changes.

In addition to the difficulty in forecasting, which poses a formidable challenge to managing market risk, lack of proper understanding of *systemic risk* has emerged as one of the key failures of current risk management. The problem is particularly potent because of the wide use of derivative products, which can propagate risk in ways difficult to understand and control. Bruce Jacobs, principal of Jacobs Levy Equity Management, said:

There has been a lot of discussion about how diversification supposedly failed during the recent credit crisis. But it seems to me that the real problem was the failure not of diversification—that is, risk sharing—but of risk shifting. Since the 1980s at least, there has been explosive growth in strategies and products that seek to reduce risk by shifting it from one or a few risk bearers to a market full of investors. This was the aim of the mortgage-backed structured products behind the 2002–06 housing bubble and a cause of its collapse in 2007–2008. Rather than assuming the risk of default on their housing loans, banks packaged the loans and sold them in the form of mortgage-backed securities [MBS].

Risk shifting also underlies most option products because option sellers have to hedge their short positions and, ultimately, rely on underlying markets to do so via dynamic hedging. Big problems can arise, however, when the risk being shifted is systemic in nature. Idiosyncratic risks can be managed by diversification; the likelihood of all or even most of the houses covered by an insurer burning down at the same time is virtually nil. The same is not true for housing *values*, as the world began to discover in 2006. Materialization of a large systemic risk that has been supposedly "insured" against is likely to result in widespread losses and lead to an increase in selling that can dry up liquidity. The insurance products and the institutions behind them can fail. Because of the linkages between various counterparties, one institution's failure may lead to systemic failure and broad economic risk.

Dr. Jacobs cited his articles on risk avoidance and market fragility (2004) and on the subprime securitization and the credit crisis (2009).

As for inadequate procedures, FactSet's Dr. Greiner put the accent on the lack of a proper risk culture. He remarked,

What 2008 did was force the discussion about moving a risk-aware firm toward becoming a risk-enabled firm and having a risk culture. Does a firm actually have a risk culture? Do they spend as much time worrying about losing money as making it? Most firms do not. . . . This leads [us] to stress-testing. Not enough teams are leveraging it. It should be emphasized in portfolio construction as much as the alpha estimate. Risk models are not used enough across mandates, and when they are, they are sometimes not understood well enough by those who "lease" them. . . . Think about it, they outsource the risk management! That tells you the level of importance it is to the firm. Moreover, risk managers do not have veto power over the portfolio, only the portfolio managers do.

Dr. Greiner identified five reasons why it is *difficult* to form a risk culture inside an asset management firm:

1. Portfolio managers are considered to be the best judge of risk–reward trade-offs.

2. Strategies are proprietary.

3. Return is the ultimate—and, in a lot of cases, the only—objective.

4. Risk management is not considered central to the success of the investment process.

5. Regulatory and compliance constraints are considered to be a drag on performance.

The importance of scenario generation in risk management was emphasized by several sources. Professor Lleo noted that Princeton's John Mulvey and the University of British Columbia's William Ziemba both recommend the use of stochastic programming to optimize asset management relative to liabilities.[17] Professor Lleo remarked,

> What we can learn from the stochastic programming culture is how to generate scenarios and how to incorporate them in our portfolio selection process. One of Professor Ziemba's key points is that it is often more important to avoid a blow-up in bad scenarios than to get the highest possible return in good scenarios.

According to Professor Lleo, scenario generation can help integrate the tools and models we now have with aspects of stress testing to develop truly "total integrated risk management."

GMO's Mr. Montier (2012) argued that risk is not a number but a permanent impairment of capital. He suggested that we should think about risk along three dimensions that damage capital: (1) valuation risk (buying an overvalued asset), (2) fundamental or real business risk, and (3) financing risk, including leverage and overcrowding (investors flocking to particular stocks).

Sources suggested that risk management calls for a greater use of common sense than was the case in the recent past. However, many remarked that common sense is not that common, especially when it goes against a person's perceived interests. Nevertheless, when financial markets and the real economy become too misaligned—as we saw, for example, with the dotcom bubble and the housing and MBS bubble—bells should start to ring. In his keynote presentation at the Third Annual CFA Institute European Investment Conference, John Kay (2010), distinguished British economist and visiting professor at the London School of Economics, added to the list

---

[17]Stochastic programming is a mathematical optimization technique based on generating scenarios. It is used for problems involving uncertainty when probability distributions governing the data are known or can be estimated. In asset management, stochastic programming is used in asset/liability management to achieve diversification and protection from extreme events. See Ziemba and Mulvey (1998).

of things that he suggests must be used together with our models. His list includes logic, judgment, intuition, probabilities, and narratives.

As for the idea that our definitions of risk are too narrow, PGGM's Jaap van Dam summed up the feeling in his observation that risk has many more dimensions than simply statistical dimensions. He said,

> I feel that, instead of "diversifying to the max," we have to learn to think about softer but, in my opinion, very important risk-mitigating factors. Factors like trust—do we really trust the companies or people we invest with; understanding—do we understand how return is being generated and what can go wrong; grip or control—if we see things developing in the wrong direction, can we influence them or can we only vote with our feet? This is a radical change versus a world in which the basic recipe is: Invest in everything because that will maximize your diversification.

Clearly, the notion of risk is being extended. Erik Valtonen, CEO of Zurich-based Blue Diamond Asset Management and former head of risk management and CIO at the Swedish buffer fund AP3, remarked, "The way risk management is applied is becoming more holistic: from narrow-minded number crunching to a broader view that includes issues like liquidity and operational risks."

Saker Nusseibeh, CEO and head of investment at Hermes Fund Managers and chairman of the 300 Club,[18] added a risk that needs to be taken into consideration: political risk. In the thought piece "Political Risk: The Impact on Investors" published by Hermes (2012), Dr. Nusseibeh noted that it has been at least two generations since investors actively looked at the problem of political risk in the context of developed markets. "They need to start," he suggested and went on to explain,

> What is clear is that we are now approaching an era when investment decisions cannot be made without incorporating political risk into the equation. The way we approach investments has to change. Long-embedded financial concepts, such as mean reversions or efficient market theory, are already lessening in importance. The investment world must wake up to the fact that we do not operate in a hermetically sealed financial system, we now live in a political economy. (pp. 4–5)

In summary, the current practice of risk management is considered by many to be inadequate:

- It uses inadequate risk measures.

---

[18]The 300 Club defines itself as a group of investment professionals who believe there is an urgent need to raise uncomfortable and fundamental questions about the foundations of the investment industry and investing. They believe that current finance and investment theory and practice fail investors when most needed. See http://www.the300club.org/.

- It is weak regarding credit risk.

- It does not take into account the fat-tailed nature of return distributions.

- It fails to cope with systemic risk.

- It fails to understand the processes that generate crises.

- It ignores some fundamental types of risk—from operational risk to geo-political risk.

Many suggest that a new level of risk culture will be needed if the effect of sharp swings in asset values is to be mitigated. The implications of these criticisms for the teaching (and practice) of risk management are discussed in later chapters.

Crises: Do We Have the Tools for Modeling Systemic Risk?

Crisis management is part of risk management, but we will now take a separate look at crises and some new ideas about how to model (if not manage) systemic risk. As mentioned in Chapter 1, Joseph Stiglitz (2013), professor of economics at Columbia University, identified approximately 100 crises worldwide in the past 30 years. We could reasonably expect, then, that some knowledge has been gained of the determinants and the evolution of crises. Sources commented, however, that, for the most part, academia and the industry have been slow to draw such lessons.

Recall that mainstream theory maintains that the economy and markets are in a state of general equilibrium; only large, unpredictable, and exogenous events can disturb this equilibrium. Attempts to explain crises not explained by mainstream theory have taken two approaches. One approach starts with the observation that economies and financial markets are unstable complex systems. That is, far from being self-correcting equilibrium systems, economies and financial markets have endogenous mechanisms that may lead to crises. The other approach can be traced back to Minsky's financial instability hypothesis: Crises are generated by an excess of money, which fuels speculation and causes asset price inflation followed by debt deflation.

The first approach, the study of financial markets as complex systems, is a natural course to explore: Complex systems are formed by many interacting units, as are markets. Interacting units form networks that exhibit thresholds of connectivity: As the probability that two agents are connected increases, one approaches the threshold where very large connected components appear. The implication is that, in practice, small differences in the density of connections—that is, the average number of mutual links of each entity—make a big difference in terms of the connected aggregates. From the point of view of risk management, clusters of connected units are an important type of aggregate. For example, clusters of banks that have borrowing/lending relationships constitute such an aggregate. Clusters of connected economic agents create systemic risk, such as when the bankruptcy of an important financial firm propagates throughout the cluster.

Andrew Haldane, executive director for financial stability of the Bank of England, said in his speech to the Financial Student Association in Amsterdam (2009),

> On 15 September 2008, Lehman Brothers filed for Chapter 11 bankruptcy in a New York courtroom in the United States. Panic ensued. Uncertainty about its causes and contagious consequences brought many financial markets and institutions to a standstill. The market for Credit Default Swaps (CDS) froze, as Lehman was believed to be counterparty to around $5 trillion of CDS contracts.
>
> Media and modern communications fed this frenzy and transmitted it across markets. Banks hoarded liquidity for fear of lending to infected banks, causing gridlock in term money markets, spreads on lower-rated companies' bonds spiked and there was an effective boycott of the remaining large US investment banks. (p. 1 of electronic document)

There was the fear that having let Lehman Brothers fail might bring down capital markets worldwide. Mr. Haldane suggested that the disintegration of the financial system might be described in terms of *network family trees*, similar to those used to describe, for example, seizures in the electricity grid, the degradation of ecosystems, or the spread of epidemics.

Researchers working in the field suggest that the formation of aggregated clusters is characteristic of financial networks. They believe that network theory will provide the tools to produce a risk measure to predict the probability that huge aggregates will appear. Among those conducting such research are Thomas Lux (2011) at the University of Kiel (Germany), where he heads a research unit on financial markets and macroeconomic activity, and Neil Johnson (2011), who heads the University of Miami's interdisciplinary group working on complexity. In the United Kingdom, network theory applied to banks and financial markets is being carried out by Mr. Haldane and Robert May, chief scientific adviser to the UK government. Haldane and May (2011) co-authored an article on banking ecosystems that appeared in *Nature*.

Relative to how systemic risk can build up in a networked financial system, Jarrod Wilcox, president of Wilcox Investment, remarked,

> In the absence of definite criteria for how much leverage to employ, short-term incentive compensation drives taking too much risk. In the absence of an understanding of basic feedback and network behavior, market participants and regulators will discount future problem accumulations. These two phenomena remind one of the old story of looking out the window at the 50th floor of the 102-story Empire State Building and seeing a man

approaching rapidly downward, flapping his arms. When asked how he was doing, he called out "So far, so good . . . ."

The second approach, traceable back to Minsky, is being pursued at the Financial Crisis Observatory at ETH Zurich.[19] With his fellow researchers, Didier Sornette, chair of Entrepreneurial Risks at ETH Zurich and head of the observatory, begins with Minsky's hypothesis that crises are generated by an excess of money, which fuels speculation and causes asset price inflation followed by debt deflation. The researchers believe that we should return to exploring the role of banks in credit creation, the benefits of certain lost forms of regulation, and the role of central banks as fighters, rather than promoters, of bubbles. The group is conducting research into how tools from nonlinear dynamics can be used to model Minsky's hypothesis.

In a 2013 interview with *FT Magazine*'s Stephen Foley, Professor Sornette observed that financial markets can be in different states of predictability and, in some states, markets may not be predictable at all. He suggests that searching for the same level of predictability in all states is a serious modeling mistake because doing so leads to "fitting noise."[20]

We consider the implications of some of these new proposals for teaching future investment professionals in later chapters.

---

[19]The Financial Crisis Observatory defines itself as a scientific platform aimed at testing and quantifying in a systematic way and on a large scale the hypothesis that financial markets exhibit a degree of inefficiency and a potential for predictability, especially during regimes when bubbles develop. For more information, see http://www.er.ethz.ch/fco.

[20]"Fitting noise" refers to the fact that a model "fits" the unpredictable part of a signal. In general, we assume that a signal is formed by a predictable part plus unpredictable noise. A model should "fit" the part that is predictable, not the unpredictable noise.

3. Teaching Finance: Can We Do Better?

In his article "Reconstructing Economics in Light of the 2007–? Financial Crisis" (2010), Benjamin Friedman, professor of political economy at Harvard University, asked,

> How should the recent financial crisis, which . . . contradicted so many central "truths" of modern economics, change how we teach our subject? What should we be telling our students, in introductory economics courses as well as in macroeconomics courses at all levels, that we are not now telling them? More generally, what lessons should we draw for how we as economists should think about the world we are trying to analyze . . . ? (p. 1)

Do we need to ask similar questions regarding how we teach finance? What should we be telling our students about our theories and our models? Do we need to teach a new investment paradigm, as some have argued? What should we include and what should we exclude from the curriculum of students whose objective is to manage other people's money, resources, and future well-being? And has anything changed since the 2007–09 financial crisis?

Among sources, the perception is that, overall, not much has changed to date. The head of human resources at a UK investment management firm remarked,

> I have noticed that maybe things are changing a bit this year, but overall, graduates in economics and finance programs are still learning the same old theory that has been proven incorrect by the recent crisis.

And there are reasons for this inertia. First, not everyone is persuaded that changes are called for. Many academics believe that the current framework is solid and needs only minor adjustments. Second, some academics believe that throwing 40 years of research out of the curriculum is not so easy; these academics are trying to gradually rebalance their approach to teaching finance. (Note that some critics of today's prevailing finance theory consider the efforts of the past 40 years to have been a waste of time.)

Alan Kirman (2012), professor emeritus of economics at the University of Aix-Marseille III and at the École des Hautes Études en Sciences Sociales, is not a defender of neoclassical economic and finance theories, but he believes that we will have to continue to teach these theories. But teaching these theories, he argued, should not prevent us

> from opening students' eyes to the difficulties and challenges our discipline faces. This, in turn, may make [students] much more enthusiastic about understanding economic phenomena and trying to analyse them rather than boring them with what they see as interminable and irrelevant technicalities. (p. 75)

The issue is clearly considered to be a very sensitive, highly political one: Many sources contacted for their views for this book said as much. Marketing considerations also enter into the problem. As business schools market their students to investment firms, they have to be careful to prepare students who have acquired the sought-after mindset and skills.

In this chapter, we report what sources had to say about changing how we teach our subject to future investment professionals. In Chapter 4, we examine changes to the curriculum that sources suggested should be made.

Is What We Are Teaching Useful?

First, given the widespread criticism of mainstream finance theory that is based on an idealization of markets, we might ask: Should we continue to teach the theories to students aspiring to work in investment management? If our financial economics and finance theories are of little practical use because they do not describe reality, is it appropriate to teach the theory to students, most of whom are in school for practical purposes?

Robert Shiller, professor of economics at Yale University, noted the tension between teaching practical economics and teaching theoretical economics. A similar tension exists in teaching finance: For example, the theory states that markets are efficient, but in practice, asset managers seek to profit from market inefficiencies. Drawing a parallel with the physical sciences, Professor Shiller (2010a) wrote,

> It should be noted that there is not a similar tension between physics and engineering, or, more narrowly, between electromagnetics and electrical engineering. If there were, one could easily imagine that some students taking a course in electricity and magnetism might complain that the field does not prepare them for the real world of electronics. (p. 407)

The difference is that in the physical sciences, the theory that is taught has been validated. People use it, for example, to engineer airplanes, and planes do not typically crash because of design errors.

Unlike the relationship between theory and practice in the physical sciences, with mainstream finance theory, the usefulness of what we teach is not in the practical applicability of mainstream models, which is poor, but (eventually) in the value of the conceptual framework. So, why teach the difficult mathematics in which the theories of general equilibrium, market efficiency, modern portfolio theory, and continuous-time asset pricing are cast? Among those mathematical techniques called for are stochastic calculus, computational methods to solve stochastic differential equations, and the mathematics of dynamic stochastic optimization—mathematics much too difficult for the average MBA student.

Teaching these mathematical methods to students who are not able to fully appreciate the pitfalls is risky. The graduates may become overconfident in their mathematical methodologies. Consider, for example, derivatives pricing or high-frequency trading, where the temptation is to deem the highly sophisticated models to be as validated as the theories of physics. They are not. The economic reality behind the complex mathematics is hidden by the complexity of the math. The risk is exacerbated by the fact that mathematical complexity is often presented as the explanation of a successful strategy. Mathematics becomes a tool to preserve the secrecy of strategies that might be based on, for example, simple principles or better sources of information.

Do We Need to Change the Way We Teach Finance Theory?

Therefore, many argue that, although our theory is imperfect (it is still in the making), it is the *way* we teach the theory that needs to change. Jacques Olivier, professor of finance and director of the master's program in finance at HEC, Paris, remarked,

> My view is that the problem with finance education lies neither in the body of knowledge (which is, of course, imperfect but at the same time rather impressive given how young the field is) nor in the topics covered but rather in the fact that finance is too often taught in too simplistic a manner. An analogy I frequently use is that financial models are like pharmaceutical drugs: They are not perfect; used correctly, they are invaluable in solving hard problems, but used incorrectly they can kill. Many business school students—or sometimes even finance practitioners—want easy-to-use models and do not want to bother about when it is right to use which model or under what set of circumstances a model that usually works will break down. It is our duty as finance professors to go beyond this natural tendency and teach about "side effects" because—keeping on with the analogy between financial models and pharmaceutical drugs—just because it may happen that the wrong drug administered to the wrong person under the wrong circumstances can kill the patient does not mean we should conclude that all drugs are useless or dangerous.

Most (not all) of our sources agreed that today's theory provides a useful framework for thinking about economic and finance problems but has limitations. For that reason, sources suggested that it be taught less inflexibly and more pragmatically.

Sébastien Lleo, NEOMA Business School professor of finance, remarked that we should teach finance "more humbly and far less dogmatically." According to him, "We have to help our students develop their critical thinking by understanding what works, what does not, when, and why." Professor Lleo added, "Theories can be helpful as a structuring tool as long as we do not convey the illusion that finance is akin to a physical science. The financial world is much messier than that!"

Jaap van Dam, head of strategy and research at the Dutch pension fund PGGM, concurred:

> I still think that we need to have the solid theoretical base, but it is equally important that the teaching comes with a warning: "just a theory." And students must be helped to see the limitations of the dogma. Much of economics is a part of social sciences—which we tend to forget—and the complexity of the society and human interaction by far exceeds the theoretical frameworks.

As noted previously, in economics and finance, the term "theory" refers to an *idealization* of an economy, of markets, or of the behavior of financial phenomena; it does not describe reality as it is. In the physical sciences, "theory" refers to a description of reality as it is. It is the *application* of physical laws to describe complex objects that might require simplifying idealizations, not the theory itself. Physical laws always hold, or if they are found not to hold, they are modified or replaced.

Are There Any Specifics We Need to Change?

Many sources consider our current theory to be imperfect and perhaps not so useful for investment management. Indeed, as one source commented, the very idea of efficient markets is in contradiction with an entire industry that earns its living promising the opposite. This section addresses specifically what our sources suggested in terms of changing the way we teach finance theory—and finance in general—to students aspiring to be investment professionals.

Teaching the General Equilibrium Theory. As discussed in Chapter 1, general equilibrium theory (GET) states that the economy and markets are in a state of general equilibrium, meaning that the market for every good and service in the economy clears at a price at which the quantity supplied equals the quantity demanded. This equilibrium can be disturbed only by large, unpredictable, and exogenous events.

The recurrence of financial crises, however, led David Romer (2013), professor of political economy at University of California, Berkeley, to conclude that financial shocks are closer to being commonplace than to being exceptional. He counted six distinct shocks in US markets during the past 30 or so years. Didier Sornette, chairman of Entrepreneurial Risks at ETH Zurich and a physicist by training, believes that because financial markets are essentially nonstationary and unstable, we are neither teaching the right concepts nor giving the appropriate tools to future investment managers. He remarked,

The most important concept that is not taught is that financial markets are *not* stationary, so that most of the econometric and statistical techniques widely in use do not work and/or are fundamentally misleading.

To address nonstationarity as well as to understand and model it, Professor Sornette advocates a combination of economic and monetary theories coupled with (complex) system theory (we will discuss these ideas in Chapter 4). Sornette and Cauwels (2012) wrote that some simple facts about financial markets can be understood without much theoretical effort and suggested that Hyman Minsky's (1992) understanding of financial instability can be enlightening.

Diversification. Although diversification is considered a sound probabilistic concept, the benefits of diversification change as market states or correlations and expected returns change. In the case of market corrections or crashes, even a well-diversified portfolio is not protected against large losses.

Dennis Logue, professor emeritus at the Tuck School of Business Administration at Dartmouth College and chairman of the board of directors of Ledyard Financial Group, remarked that in his experience, although students are taught about diversification, they are not taught what might be done when the correlations among markets grow closer to 1 and diversification does not work (or, as defenders of diversification would argue, works less well). Students are not taught, he added, how to deal with chaos or nonnormal distributions. How we teach diversification is another illustration of the fact that, as our finance theory holds to GET, we are not preparing students to handle events outside the theory.

Professor Olivier remarked, "I do not think that one should teach diversification and Markowitz's theory without talking about structural breaks and estimation errors of the variance–covariance matrix and their implication for the composition of efficient portfolios." Steven Greiner, director of portfolio risk at FactSet Research Systems, concurs. He believes that we should be focusing on how to reduce estimation error, how to account for fat-tail correlations, and how to apply extreme-event stress testing.

Professor Sornette goes a bit farther. He believes that the concept of diversification is intrinsically inapplicable to financial markets because of their nonstationary nature.

Pricing Assets and the CAPM. Despite the critiques that the CAPM is a flawed partial equilibrium theory and the one-factor model is sloppy econometrics, and despite the fact that the tenets of the CAPM have been invalidated in numerous empirical studies, the CAPM is still widely taught as a theoretical framework for asset pricing.

But should we continue to teach the CAPM? Jim Liew, assistant professor of finance at the Johns Hopkins Carey Business School, remarked that, although the CAPM can break down in situations of distress,

> You do not throw out all of finance. Rather, you show its limitations. Students need to know the development of how models progressed, from CAPM to three- and four-factor models. As a professor in finance, you need to lay out all sides of the arguments, to paint a rich picture of the developments in context, to show the spectrum of arguments (pro and con) out there, and to ultimately encourage students to arrive at their own conclusions. CAPM is not the only thing out there.

Model risk is particularly serious in the domain of option pricing: Derivatives contracts can be complex to describe mathematically and have many distributions that need to be jointly estimated. In addition, market prices of derivative products are often set by models. In other words, derivatives are priced and traded as a function of the outcomes of complex mathematical models. As other traders try to exploit arbitrage opportunities ultimately generated by the interplay between different models, model risk is clearly a serious issue in derivatives pricing. Professor Olivier believes that option pricing should not be taught without spending time on the issue of model risk.

Dr. Greiner observed that some of the theories learned in the classroom are being applied by students when they move into investment management positions despite the empirical evidence proving that the theories are wrong. He remarked, "For instance, what MBA schools do to a fault is to tie the fundamentals of a company to the return of its stock too much. It is just not that sticky." The problem is that by teaching idealizations that are empirically unsatisfactory, we are producing a generation of students who will tend to blindly apply methodologies that are, in the end, contradicted by empirical facts.

A more fundamental critique of the academic emphasis on asset-pricing models came from Professor Lleo, who questions today's focus on precise asset pricing as opposed to pragmatic decision making. He argued that asset pricing is an intellectual exercise; focusing on decision making forces one to think pragmatically and gives priority to forecasting and uncertainty. Professor Lleo remarked,

> The rapid development of financial markets over the last 40 years has led to a shift in emphasis away from decision making and towards asset pricing. Part of the problem we face today is that asset pricing in general—and derivatives pricing in particular—gives the impression that the price of any asset can be determined unambiguously and (almost) scientifically. By centering around the decision-related aspects, we will be able to change our emphasis to what we do not know rather than what we know or think we know. It will also be easier to present our body of knowledge as heuristic

rules, rather than scientific results. Hopefully, this will help keep the field open and growing while ensuring that practitioners and academics exercise proper judgment.

Others also commented on overdependence on a theoretical framework as opposed to a practical framework for asset valuation. Referring to economic and finance theory as taught today, Russell Napier, a consultant with CLSA Asia-Pacific Markets and author of *The Anatomy of the Bear* (2005), commented,

> We should say: "Here is the intellectual framework as a starting point to establishing value." The theory is simple and not too important as it provides only a framework for the practical business of assessing value. So much of the job in assessing value relates to the future, where a theoretical framework can only be of limited use. A study of the history of valuation at least has the advantage of alerting investors to the factors that have impacted valuation and thus might do so again.

The fact that today's finance theory does not describe real markets explains why practitioners and academics who seek empirical verification of the theory are in search of a different type of theory, one that is more in line with the paradigm of the physical sciences and, therefore, of practical use. For example, Andrew Ang, professor of business at Columbia Business School, considers factor theory central to asset management. He believes that understanding factors is the key to understanding returns. He argues that factors are to assets what nutrients are to food, with factor risks the driving force behind risk premiums. Professor Ang lists as examples of investable factors interest rates, value–growth investing, volatility investing (through options, for example), and momentum portfolios as well as fundamental macro factors, such as inflation and economic growth.

That the reality of markets should be the primary object of study is perhaps the key adjustment that needs to be made to both the theory and the teaching of finance. Students now learn idealized markets where prices follow a theoretical asset-pricing model. When markets present deviations from the idealized behavior, student of finance are told that market prices tend to revert (rapidly) to their theoretical real prices. This is questionable. As one source at an investment management firm remarked, the firm gets calls from doctoral students who typically want to come and give presentations on what they have discovered to be market "anomalies" (that is, mispricings), but the anomalies, he notes, are not linked to what happened in 2007–2009—a very big anomaly indeed!

The Efficient Market Hypothesis. In response to the question: Should we continue to teach EMH (and other theories such as GET and CAPM) to students of investment management, sources mentioned the need to encourage students to be skeptical of the theory we are teaching. With reference to the theory of market efficiency, Professor Logue remarked,

> Students are not taught to be skeptical enough. If the professor says markets are efficient, they do not really know how to produce a study refuting this—or to design a study that would fail to refute it if that is the result they would get.

The EMH argues in favor of investing in passive indices as opposed to active management. But, as sources remarked, a whole industry bets on active management. Edward Qian, CIO and head of multiasset research at PanAgora, commented,

> The teaching of finance and economics places much emphasis on equilibrium theory and efficient market hypothesis. But active management is based on finding mispricing and/or forecasting future returns. If someone has a strong belief in EMH, it is unlikely that he or she will be motivated to find evidence that rebukes EMH and, therefore, less likely to be successful. Of course, some students go on to be successful professional investors. The irony is that while they are profiting from market inefficiencies, their professors are publishing scholarly articles—and, in some cases, winning the Nobel Prize in Economic Sciences—with ideas of rational expectations and market equilibrium.

Some argue that the importance of the EMH is being overstated. Mr. Napier asked, "Should we continue to teach such concepts as the EMH, GET, CAPM?" His suggestion:

> Take the theory as a skeleton of the body and do not make too much of it. If one is a medical student, one needs to know the skeleton—but do not spend too much time on it; it does not tell you how the body works. The theory is based on assumptions that were put there for good reasons, but many of these assumptions can lead to a certainty of conclusions that are both illusory and dangerous.

Risk Measurement and Risk Management. Risk measurement came under criticism for the inadequacy of the risk measures commonly used in investment management (prevalently VaR and its focus on normal distributions), and risk management, for the narrow scope of the risks it defines (commonly limited to a statistical measurement of market risk).

Professor Lleo, among others, questions the focus on normal distributions. He noted,

> A common confusion about market behavior stems from the fact that many of the applications presented in courses and books focus on the normal distribution. We have known for years—at least since Mandelbrot in the early 1960s—that the normal distribution is not a good model of asset behavior, but we still develop most of our examples around it because it is easy

for the students to understand and only requires very limited knowledge of probability and statistics. A remedy would be to strengthen the treatment of quantitative methods so that academics can confidently show students other types of examples and models. Academics and an increasing number of practitioners do have the knowledge, yet going beyond normality is still not part of the standard portfolio management curriculum.

This sentiment was expressed by others even before the financial crisis that began in the summer of 2007. In the preface to *Fat-Tailed and Skewed Asset Return Distributions* (Rachev et al. 2005), the authors wrote,

> The theory and practice of finance draws heavily on probability theory. All MBA programs prepare finance majors for their career in the profession by requiring one generalist course in probability theory and statistics, populated by all business majors. While several probability distributions are covered in the course, the primary focus is on the normal or Gaussian distribution. Students find it easy to understand and apply the normal distribution: Give them the expected value and standard deviation and probability statements about outcomes can be easily made. . . .

> Armed with this rudimentary knowledge of probability theory, finance students march into their elective courses in finance that introduce them to the quantitative measures of risk (the standard deviation) and the quantitative inputs needed to implement modern portfolio theory (the expected value or mean and the standard deviation). In listing assumptions for most theories of finance, the first assumption on the list is often: "Assume asset returns are normally distributed." The problem, however, is that empirical evidence does not support the assumption that many important variables in finance follow a normal distribution. (p. xi)

Charles Chang, associate professor and director of the Master of Finance program at the Shanghai Advanced Institute of Finance, believes we are not teaching students a broad enough range of risk measures. He notes that, although the largest collapses of the last two decades or so (Long-Term Capital Management and the subprime mortgage crisis) were in fixed-income markets, most of the literature (especially the investment texts) focuses on equity markets and two-tailed risk. He argues that credit risk evaluation, collapse models, and cross-market contagion should be more widely taught.

Finally, as regards the narrow definition of risk, we have noted that macroeconomic and geopolitical risk are also now on the radar screens of investment managers. Saker Nusseibeh (2012), CEO and head of investment at Hermes Fund Managers, believes that such economic variables as GDP and interest rates have become too shallow as measures of a country's risk–reward profile; he suggests that we need to take into consideration, among others, the actions of politicians.

Crises. The potential impact of a crisis on a portfolio can be enormous, but crises do not have a place in mainstream finance's GET. No investment strategy based on mainstream finance theory can, therefore, protect investors from market-wide crashes.

Nevertheless, crises do occur. Friedman (2012) noted that too many supposed six-standard-deviation (or even ten-standard-deviation) events have occurred within recent decades for them to be considered six-standard-deviation events any longer. He argues that once this instability is recognized, the methodologies for managing assets change fundamentally.

A key theory of market instability was described by Hyman Minsky (see, for example, his *Stabilizing an Unstable Economy*, 1986). Minsky's financial instability hypothesis is conceptually straightforward: The generation of excessive money produces asset inflation, which in turn, creates instabilities that can lead to a crisis.

Attempts are being made to develop Minsky's ideas into a comprehensive theory of market instabilities based on the theory of complex systems. ETH Zurich's Professor Didier Sornette argues that crises are predictable in a probabilistic sense and that a number of "signatures" of oncoming crises can be recognized, including a faster-than-exponential growth rate of financial assets.

Do such theories have a place in programs that are forming risk managers? As Professor Friedman (2012) remarked, abandoning the rational expectations assumption would be "deeply subversive," but "[m]ispricing of assets and subsequent losses for their holders matter in themselves" (pp. 125–126).

In summary, most sources believe that today's mainstream theories will continue to be taught, at least as a framework for thinking, for several reasons. One is that no all-encompassing alternative theory exists. Another reason is that much competitive pressure is on schools to form students with a body of knowledge close to what is expected—the "dominant thinking." Most sources note that the teaching of mainstream theories should be less dogmatic and point out potential pitfalls.

Finally, attitudes toward crises and how to teach them can be placed in one school or another. According to one school of thinking, primarily the school advocating mainstream finance, crises are generated by unpredictable exogenous events; modern economies and markets recover rapidly from crises, so crises are not a major subject of concern. According to the other school, crises are viewed as endogenous events caused by the accumulation of internal tensions—in particular, an excess generation of money. This school of thought holds that the probability of crises can be assessed and that, therefore, the dynamics of crises should be an integral part of the teaching for future investment professionals.

Exhibit 3.1 summarizes these conclusions.

Exhibit 3.1. Summary of Opinions on the Teaching of Mainstream Finance and Investment Management Theory

Subject Taught	Fundamentally Correct	Fundamentally Wrong but Useful	Fundamentally Wrong and Useless
Mainstream economic and finance theory	Because mainstream theory is fundamentally correct, empirically faithful, and useful, mainstream theory and the conceptual framework behind it should continue to be taught.	Although mainstream theory is an idealization that does not describe reality as it is, it offers a useful framework for thinking and should, therefore, continue to be taught, albeit with a warning: "only a theory."	Despite the fact that mainstream theory is an idealization that does not describe reality as it is, there is no all-encompassing competing theory to teach. When it is taught, however, students should be made aware of its limitations and lack of empirical validation.
Capital asset pricing model	The CAPM is a fundamental model that should be taught.	The CAPM has been empirically falsified but remains conceptually important and should be taught, if only for its historical importance in the development of asset-pricing models.	The CAPM has been invalidated by numerous empirical studies and is fundamentally misleading, so it should not be taught except as regards its place in the history of asset-pricing theory.
Asset-pricing theories (APTs)	APTs are a great achievement of modern finance theory and are central to the teaching of finance.	Although empirically weak, APTs provide a useful conceptual framework for students of finance.	APTs are based on considering an infinite stream of future cash flows and, therefore, are not based on observables; nevertheless, despite being scientifically weak, APTs have their place in curricula as providing a common language until we have a new, more scientifically based theory.
Efficient market hypothesis	The EMH is at the foundation of finance theory; it is almost a self-evident truth and a "must" in any finance program.	The EMH is based on a solid conceptual foundation but, in practice, is subject to important anomalies; it places the burden on active managers to show they are finding anomalies; inefficient pricing should not be assumed. The EMH should be taught but critically.	The EMH is void of meaning; the notion of theoretical prices is not based on observables. The EMH should be replaced by the notion of market forecastability and be taught as such.

(Continued)

Exhibit 3.1. Summary of Opinions on the Teaching of Mainstream Finance and Investment Management Theory (Continued)

Subject Taught	Fundamentally Correct	Fundamentally Wrong but Useful	Fundamentally Wrong and Useless
Risk	Risk is an important concept and is well understood, but many market events are completely unpredictable and escape risk measurement. Risk should be taught within the framework of mainstream theory.	Current (market) risk measures are inadequate; in most cases, they miss extreme events. New risk measures that take into consideration, for example, fat tails should be taught. In addition, more attention should be given to credit and liquidity risk.	Current tools miss many important risk events, including systemic risk and geopolitical risk. Teaching should bring these risks to the forefront.
Crises	Crises are generated by unpredictable exogenous events. Modern economies and markets recover rapidly from crises, so the latter are not a major subject for teaching.	Crises are endogenous events caused by the accumulation of internal tensions—in particular, the excessive generation of money. The probability of crises can be assessed, and the dynamics of crises should be a fundamental part of the teaching for future investment professionals.	

Even though today's mainstream thinking is likely to remain dominant for some time, at least as a framework, a rebalancing is going on. As discussed in upcoming chapters, educators are confronting the demand to broaden the curriculum and encourage critical, out-of-the-box thinking. In that regard, the most recent financial crisis has had an impact.

4. What's Missing in the Curricula for Future Investment Professionals?

We asked sources what, in the wake of the most recent financial crisis, they thought needed to be reinforced, introduced, or reintroduced in programs preparing students for jobs in investment management. In reporting their responses, we will distinguish where necessary between suggestions for MBA curricula and suggestions for curricula in finance-oriented PhD programs.

First, let's address time constraints. A typical MBA program is two years. Some sources commented that a two-year program to prepare students for jobs in investment management is already quite packed and that finding the time to introduce new material is not easy. Dennis Logue, professor emeritus at the Tuck School of Business Administration at Dartmouth College and chairman of the board of directors of Ledyard National Bank, said, "It is tough to figure out how to cram all that a professional investor should know into a typical two-year MBA program." Indeed, sources agreed that such a program is just the start. Forming a professional investor requires years of on-the-job experience. Among the human resources managers we talked to, most said that their firms run intensive induction programs for new recruits, after which graduates are assigned to a team with coaching. Only after years of on-the-job training are these employees given more responsibility.

In PhD programs in finance, the main concern is that students develop too narrow a focus on mastering difficult mathematical methods. This challenge is time-consuming and leaves little or no time for developing broader knowledge of economics and finance.

Any educational program can be said to be a compromise between time constraints and the great number of topics that could be covered. For that reason, human resources managers and professional headhunters that we talked to strongly suggested that recruits continue their professional education once on the job. Doing so shows commitment to the job, and because of the fast pace of change in the world of finance, from the point of view of markets, products, and technology, no body of knowledge can be considered definitive.

Another problem that arises in discussing the curriculum is the diversity of roles and jobs for which students should be prepared. Harvard University professor of economics Edward Glaeser (2012) considered the wide range of roles played by market participants to be the great challenge in educating investment professionals. Is there any common body of knowledge that should be shared among these market participants and thus should be reflected in the curriculum?

Sébastien Lleo, NEOMA Business School professor of finance, commented on what he called the silos separating the various areas and functions in finance:

> I have encountered many forms of finance: empirical finance, financial economics, financial accounting/financial statement analysis, asset valuation, corporate finance, quantitative finance, financial mathematics/mathematical finance, computational finance and even econophysics. I am less concerned about the subspecialization that appears in finance (corporate finance, finance, math/quant finance, behavioral sciences in finance . . .[21]) than about the knowledge gap that these narrow fields leave in their wake.

He added,

> My observation—after spending some years in the industry, in a mathematics department, and now in a business school—is that there is a sizable knowledge gap between business-oriented management, finance-oriented operations, and quantitatively oriented trading and risk management. This knowledge gap feeds a much wider cultural gap between the various areas and functions. Combined, these gaps can have disastrous consequences, as evidenced by the various mishaps at UBS.

In considering what knowledge needs to be shared across silos, for example, Charles Chang, associate professor and director of the Master of Finance program at the Shanghai Advanced Institute of Finance, remarked that, whatever one's specific field or strategy in investment management, everyone can learn from cross-training in various specialties—for example, hedge funds. He said,

> I think a full discussion of popular hedge fund strategies is important. This is not because they are necessarily profitable but because these tools are now at investors' disposal all over the world. They need to know how to use them, what can be done, and what is risky to try. Cross-hedge risk, maturity risk, etc., are more important than ever, as is the role of the yield curve slope in hedging and strategies—once again on the fixed-income side.

> I think it is particularly important to point out differences in processes, trading methodologies, and regulations in different economies. Again, this is not so that students can learn specifically how to invest in, say, Korea, but rather so that they will know what to look for no matter what market they may be trading.

Didier Sornette, chair of Entrepreneurial Risks at ETH Zurich, believes that whatever area the student wants to enter, each student can profit from learning a systems approach, nonstationarity, and the economics of incentives, of asymmetrical information, and of various market failures. Sornette's ideas are part of the larger argument against neoclassical finance's emphasis

---

[21]The list of course is not exhaustive and might include, for example, real estate, insurance, and government and infrastructure finance.

on theories and models not based on empirical evidence. The argument is that finance theory needs to make a transition from what John Kay (2012), British economist and visiting professor at the London School of Economics, described as "a deductive approach, which draws conclusions from a group of axioms, and whose empirical relevance depends entirely on the universal validity of the axioms" (p. 53) to an empirical science. The theory of systems—in particular, the theory of complex systems—might just prove to be a fruitful avenue for this endeavor (see the section on crises in Chapter 2 for a discussion of complex systems).

Specific Topics to Reinforce or Add

We asked sources what subjects they believed should be reinforced in or added to the curriculum. The subjects most mentioned are, in order of the number of times they were cited, as follows:

- macroeconomics,

- a historical perspective on macroeconomics,

- the history of financial markets and economic history,

- behavioral finance,

- statistics beyond the use of the normal distribution,

- risk management, and

- ethics.

The Need for (More) Macroeconomics. When asked what they looked for in recruits, the human resources manager at a large continental European fund management firm replied,

> Good macroeconomic understanding. We expect our fund managers to be able to reason on the impact on their portfolios of, for example, a rise in the price of rice in Southeast Asia or the results in recent Italian elections. We want good economic thinking, an understanding of macro and political. In the recruiting process, we involve business managers a lot to challenge candidates—and some can be very tough. We are interested in understanding candidates' economic thinking.

Good economic thinking came up often in conversations and the literature. Andrew Haldane (2012), executive director for financial stability at the Bank of England, identified what he called an "intellectual virus" at the root of the most recent financial crisis—that is, "analytical failure" (p. 133).

Most of our sources—both practitioners and academics—share the opinion that macroeconomics needs to be reinforced in the curriculum of students of investment management. Recent interest in macroeconomics and its history is likely a reaction to the recent financial crisis and how it surprised so many in the finance world. Professor Chang remarked, "I believe the macro effects are most important and enjoy the weakest coverage of almost any area."

Edward Qian, CIO and head of research for multiasset portfolios at quantitative fund manager PanAgora, agreed:

> The global financial crisis and its aftermath prove the importance of macroeconomics in active management. Yet, most students from economics and finance programs seem to have little exposure to macroeconomic theory. They often focus on certain anomalies of capital markets. This is akin to missing the forest for the trees. Maybe this is because standard macroeconomic theory is being challenged by recurring financial crises. While there is fierce debate among economists about various approaches or ideologies of macroeconomics, it would be beneficial to students to have more exposure in macroeconomics and its related fields, such as interest rates, exchange rates, inflation, etc. Unfortunately, we have seen few students with knowledge in these areas.

These comments apply to students who will seek a career as, for example, a portfolio manager as well as to PhD students who aspire to becoming quants, for example, on systemic management teams, in risk management, or in trading/execution. The tendency is for the current generation of PhD students to be excessively focused on technical details, on prowess in discovering subtle profit opportunities in financial markets. This tendency is exacerbated by the diffusion of high-frequency trading and stories of the fortunes made in high-frequency trading as well as in managing hedge funds.

Clearly, the type of macroeconomics we are discussing is not the formalism and mathematics of general equilibrium theory. A widely held belief among our sources is that much economic reasoning must remain *qualitative*. Professor Kay (2007) commented that, rather than make "sharp predictions," perhaps the best that we can do is to identify qualitative regularities and patterns in events, which, if we accept our inability to make sharp predictions, can allow us to gain much in the way of useful knowledge. He wrote, "We will never know what an exchange rate will be two years from now, . . . but we can look to purchasing power and capital flows for guidance" (pp. 1–2).

One aspect of macroeconomic thinking that should be emphasized is the recognition that economies can move through different states, so understanding and forecasting the *transition* to and from different states is vital in asset management. Commenting on the need for more macroeconomic reasoning, Evariste Lefeuvre (2012), CIO and chief economist for the Americas at Natixis Global Asset Management, wrote:

> Macroeconomic views (or insights) should replace predictions because, as the portfolio management industry focuses more on risks, it has to accept a

more uncertain world in which regime shifts can only be assessed by a mix of judgments and nonquantitative macro/markets analysis. In a nonlinear world, "adaptation" is the key word. (p. 2)

From the point of view of modeling, identifying economic states is quite challenging. It requires a special type of reasoning because introducing economic states requires long time series and can easily produce an explosion in the number of parameters to be estimated.

Another aspect that argues for greater attention being paid to macroeconomics is the growing role of governments in economies and markets. Professor Chang remarked, "Regulation and different levels of government intervention are applied in different countries. The role of policy is very important, both in crisis avoidance and recovery."

Indeed, sources commented that in the wake of the 2007–09 financial crisis and ensuing Great Recession, the increased role of governments and the impact of government policy on markets have reinforced the need among students for macroeconomic reasoning. Jaap van Dam, the Dutch pension fund PGGM's head of strategy and research, said,

> If you look back at the past 30 years, the economy was largely independent of the political picture, but now, if you look at the economy, it is especially the political economy that one must look at. It goes beyond the Fed's quantitative easing; you must look at free trade and its effects.

Mr. Van Dam added that because of the need to protect their economies and jobs, governments may be forced to abandon many of the tenets of today's dominating economic thought, including free trade.

This comment takes the discussion beyond macroeconomics in the direction of political economics. Saker Nusseibeh (2012), CEO and head of investment at Hermes Fund Manager, remarked that for decades, asset managers have ignored the political landscape but said that doing so is no longer possible. Dr. Nusseibeh believes that increased conflicts and an era of politically motivated economic intervention mean that politics and economics are so intertwined that we can no longer study the two in isolation. Asset managers, he argues, must understand what the changing political environment means for the asset classes they invest in.

Another compelling reason for reinforcing macroeconomic teaching in the curriculum is the fact that, in the end, the economy drives financial markets. Professor Lleo remarked, "Macroeconomics and microeconomics are the foundation rock of investment management. The markets cannot stay disconnected very long from the actual state of the economy." When financial markets follow paths disconnected from the economy—witness the recent housing bubble in the United States—the way is paved for a crisis. A disconnect between economies and financial markets generally implies that financial profits are being created artificially, thus creating a situation of instability.

A Historical Perspective on Macroeconomics. Although our sources generally considered the teaching of macroeconomics to be fundamental to investment management, many noted that simply reinforcing macroeconomics in the curriculum is not sufficient. Sources also mentioned the need to teach a historical perspective on macroeconomics.

Robert Shiller (2010a), professor of economics at Yale University, wrote,

> The ephemeral nature of macroeconomic models is, I feel, an essential problem with the subject matter. [Mainstream] macroeconomics seeks simple ways of thinking about highly complex phenomena that cannot really be taken apart and studied in a systematic way. The models will always be being discarded and reformulated for that reason, as economic events make it seem urgent to change the assumptions of the models to reflect elementary reality. As teachers of macroeconomics, we have to live with that reality. I think that means that we have to respect alternative ways of understanding macroeconomics and that we keep a long historical perspective on the history of economic thought.
>
> For me, alternative views that must be incorporated into our teaching include those promoted by the other social sciences: psychology, sociology, political science, and anthropology. For me, maintaining a proper perspective on alternative views means also incorporating historical analysis, real historical analysis such as that which proceeds in our history departments, into our teaching about economics. For me, too, we also must keep in view the fundamental importance of institutions—our established organizations, practices, and laws—and remind our students that these must be taken into account before judging any economic model. (p. 407)

As we have had occasion to mention previously, economics is not about studying laws of nature; it is about studying the behavior of an ever changing human artifact. By understanding how economic behavior changed in the past as different economic structures materialized, students gain a deeper and broader intellectual perspective on today's economic thought. This brings us to what sources had to say about the relevance of considering other social sciences, starting with the history of financial markets and the history of the economy, economics, and economic thought.

The History of Finance/Financial Markets. Together with the need to reinforce the study of macroeconomics, the subject matter most frequently mentioned as missing from most curricula for future investment professionals is the history of finance and of financial markets. Teaching the history of finance and of financial markets, sources believe, would give students a long-term perspective.

Russell Napier, author of *The Anatomy of the Bear* (2009) and lecturer on the history of financial markets at Edinburgh Business School, commented,

> Financial history gives you a range of the possible. It gives you rules in the same way that any sport has rules. The rules are the way that markets have worked which, as in sports, narrow the outcomes but still leave room for numerous different outcomes.

The need for aspiring investment professionals to study the history of financial markets was recognized by the CFA Society of the UK (2011) in a report that castigates "financial amnesia" among market players and regulators. The report argued that such financial amnesia "causes risk to be mispriced, bubbles to develop, and crises to break" (p. 2).

PanAgora's Dr. Qian said,

> If one thinks finance and economics are to some degree a social science, then the study of history is an integral part of education. This is especially true for an investor. For instance, if one reads *This Time Is Different* by [Carmen] Reinhart and [Kenneth] Rogoff [2009], then one might have second thoughts about market equilibrium. If one reads *Lords of Finance: The Bankers Who Broke the World* by [Liaquat] Ahamed [2009], one would have some understanding of the effects of monetary policy after a financial crisis better than any model can provide.
>
> Another example is the low-volatility phenomenon, which is one piece of empirical evidence against the capital asset pricing model. Fischer Black, together with others, actually discovered the low-volatility anomaly in the early 1970s, soon after CAPM was conceived.

In arguing for adding a section on the history of the economy and financial markets in finance programs, Professor Lleo remarked,

> We can learn many insights from past crises and disasters, and these events also provide a wonderful illustration of the importance of key concepts such as proper asset and liability management and the impact of market illiquidity. Crises such as Long-Term Capital Management and the Asian crisis were not so long ago. Yet, very few—probably fewer than 1% or 2%—of my executive education students were working in finance at that time. If they did not live through it, then we need to show it to them.

Studying the history of financial markets also helps students understand the effect of "financial euphoria" on markets. Although other elements are needed to form a bubble—in particular, excessive money generation—euphoria is a key component in bubble formation. The temptation for asset managers to jump on rising stocks or industries or rising markets is hard to resist because clients may believe they are losing out on profit opportunities. The 1997–2000 dot-com bubble is a good example: Asset managers who were skeptical of the pricing of dot-com stocks either reluctantly included these stocks in their port-folios or saw clients walk away. James Montier (2012), a member of fund manager GMO's asset allocation team, advocated that all investors be required to study the history of financial euphoria:

> It never ceases to amaze me how little we learn from one crisis to another. [John Kenneth] Galbraith noted "the extreme brevity of financial memory." The details of each bubble may change but the underlying patterns (usually involving some nasty combination of illiquidity and leverage) do not. We had seen instruments like CDOs before. During the junk bond boom of the late 1990s, they were collateralized bond obligations. (pp. 11–12)

Among his suggested reading list for students, Professor Logue includes Charles Kindleberger and Robert Aliber's *Manias, Panics, and Crashes* (1978) and Charles Mackay's classic *Extraordinary Popular Delusions and the Madness of Crowds* (1841). Mackay describes the South Sea Company bubble (1711–1720), the Mississippi Company bubble (1719–1720), and the Dutch "tulip mania" of the early seventeenth century.

Using history as a source of patterns, however, requires discipline. Princeton University professor of history and international affairs Harold James (2012) cautioned,

> A simple-minded application of historical lessons . . . does not offer self-evident patterns. . . . The best way of thinking about history is as a way of testing conventional hypotheses—particularly when those hypotheses are being used to create market opportunities (by building false confidence, but also by engendering exaggerated despair). Conventional thinking offers—in financial debates as in others—a primrose path to perdition. Clio's task is to show us that it is not the only path available.[22] (p. 90)

The history of financial markets was mentioned by many sources, but the need to study the markets themselves was also underlined. Alan Kirman (2012), professor emeritus of economics at the University of Aix-Marseille III and at the École des Hautes Études en Sciences Sociales, suggested that we should rethink the nature of our courses. (He was referring to economics, but his remarks are equally relevant to finance.) An obvious idea, he said, would be to teach a course on markets but not a course that simply describes their role as efficient allocators of resources. He suggested that such a course should encompass what markets are, how they operate, and how they have evolved. He added,

> It would be easy and informative to teach a course in which one would sur-vey the role of markets in history, their different institutions and how they

---

[22]In Greco-Roman mythology, each of the nine muses, all daughters of Zeus and Mnemosyne (Memory), were thought to preside over one of the nine recognized arts or sciences. Clio is the muse of history.

function for different commodities. The student would also find out, for example, how the stock exchange works and how prices are formed there, how the order book works and so forth. (p. 72)

At the Yale School of Management, the International Center for Finance has had a financial history initiative for the past decade.[23] The center has been collecting, disseminating, analyzing, and publishing data and documents from the history of world finance during that time. William Goetzmann, the center's director and professor of finance and management studies at the Yale School of Management, commented,[24]

Studying the history of finance is necessary to understanding its essential nature. While the financial crisis of 2008 alerted many to the need for history as a measure and model of crises, the study of financial innovation through time provides a much richer perspective. History teaches important lessons about how finance can change society.

What contracting problems did the first corporations solve? What went wrong when paper money first appeared in China? How have mortgages been used to back securities in other time periods? What happens to the equity markets when serious recessions and social crises occur? Studying the how and why of financial institutions, markets and instruments forces us to understand modern finance in the broader context of human lives. It provides a framework for understanding how finance can make the world better and what kinds of possibilities and problems can emerge. Basic questions from the past offer insights into modern conditions.

The History of Economics/Economic Thought. Some sources underlined the need to include the history of economics and/or of economic thought in the curricula. Not everyone agreed on this point. Some argued that economists have not yet sorted the two competing schools of thought, but others remarked that studying different schools of thought broadens students' perspectives.

Professor Lleo remarked that limiting the teaching of finance theory to mathematical models deprives students of key understanding. Noting that past market bubbles and crises are powerful reminders that the world is more complex than suggested by finance theory, he said, "One striking observation is that economic thinking seems to have gotten poorer in some aspects just as it got more structured and precise in others." Referring to Frank Knight's (1921) distinction between risk and uncertainty and to John Maynard Keynes' (1936) description of the "animal spirits" of markets and entrepreneurs, Professor Lleo

---

[23]For more information on the Yale School of Management's International Center for Finance, see http://som.yale.edu/faculty-research/our-centers-initiatives/international-center-finance.
[24]In *The Great Mirror of Folly: Finance, Culture, and the Crash of 1720* (2013), Goetzmann, Catherine Labio, Geert Rowenhorst, Timothy Young, and Robert Shiller study the bursting of the first global stock market bubble in 1720.

added, "Yet, finance theory tells us a different story: Uncertainty can be viewed as idiosyncratic risk and can be diversified away. The only source of return should be related to market risk premia and the scaling of risk exposure."

Mohamed El-Erian, former CEO and co-CIO of PIMCO, with US$1.97 trillion in assets under management, said in an interview with *Business Insider* (Ro 2012) that even as a child, he was frequently prompted to read different interpretations of the same set of facts. Referring specifically to his education as an economist, he said,

> Economics at Cambridge in the late 1970s was not about seeing the world in a particular way. Instead, it was about gaining familiarity with four schools of thought—from neoclassical to Marxist, and from Keynesian to neo-Ricardian.

Dr. El-Erian went on to describe the benefits of such an education:

> Critically, the emphasis went well beyond answering the question of the day. It was also about gaining a broad range of analytical tools to dissect it, explore it, and extend it into even more meaningful territory. Put another way, "how" you thought about a problem was as important as the "what" of the solution.

Note that in this comment, economic theory and political economics overlap. Economic schools of thought, from Marxism to Keynesian to the neoclassical, differ not only in theory but also in their views of society. Different economic systems are not different theories of the same economic object. Actually, they describe different societal objectives, different visions of the allocation of resources. Of course, this fact complicates the study of economics because theory is intertwined with political considerations. But as Professor Kay (2012) remarked, economic behavior, theories, and models are "context specific" (p. 52).

The need to study economic history—or the history of economic thought—to broaden one's ability to analyze financial phenomena was commented on by many sources. In a letter to the *Financial Times*, Michael Oliver (2008), a senior lecturer in finance at the Open University and cofounder and director of the firm Global Partnership Family Offices, wrote the following in response to a letter in the *Financial Times* bemoaning the weak impact of economists in financial institutions:

> The more fundamental issue to be addressed is why economists are not taken seriously. Over the past 20 years I have watched in despair as universities and business schools have grilled students with existence theorems and trained them to be competent in mathematics as mathematicians are, frequently at the expense of understanding how the real-world macroeconomy works. This situation has been made worse by the demise of economic history in the curriculum, a subject that not only contextualises contemporary

problems, but also helps economists think more broadly. There is no substitute for rigour, but we need to ask ourselves whether we are being too rigorous about the wrong things and leaving the finance industry all the poorer because of it.

Stephen King (2012), group chief economist and head of economics and asset allocation research at HSBC, also lamented the lack of a historical perspective:

> Too few economists newly arriving in the financial world have any real knowledge of events that, while sometimes in the distant past, may have tremendous relevance for current affairs. Admittedly, these events (e.g., the 1929 crash, the Great Depression, the 1907 crash) are not easy to analyze using modern-day mathematical and statistical techniques: The pre-computer world has its limitations too. There is no reason, however, to limit economic understanding to what can readily be downloaded into a spreadsheet with n degrees of freedom. A more imaginative approach is required, if only to expand the mind beyond what can be immediately sliced and diced in different statistical ways. Economic history can enlighten, in particular by emphasizing the social and political forces that lead to economic booms and busts. Economists should not be slaves to economic data that reflect only the most recent experience. (p. 22)

Comments similar to King's are not heard in the physical sciences. The history of the development of physics is a subject of study in itself, but it does not shed much light on contemporary physics. The reason is that physics is a highly developed discipline with a rigorous empirical validation process. The problem of mainstream economic and finance theory is its divorce from reality, which makes it all but irrelevant for practical applications, such as asset management.

The history of financial economics is relevant also because it would allow us to build a theory based on empirical data, although, as Dr. King remarked, we have fewer data to run through our spreadsheets the farther back we go in time. Nevertheless, the speed of change was slower in the past, and we might take a coarse-grained view of past economic and finance data.

Professor Shiller (2010a) commented on student dissatisfaction with the teaching of economics—particularly macroeconomics—during the current financial crisis because of its irrelevance to the situation at hand. He remarked,

> The economics profession seems unusual, when compared with some other professions, in complaints that the teaching is irrelevant to practical lives. There appear to be few complaints among physics students that their education does not prepare them for practical pursuits, such as engineering. But economics, particularly macroeconomics, is different from physics not because of the mode of teaching, but because the subject matter is harder to conceptualize. Models have to be frequently discarded and fundamentally new ones have to be brought to bear to make them relevant to changed circumstances. (p. 403)

Professor Shiller suggested that by regularly and respectfully referring to the history of economic thought, students might understand "the reasons for the theoretical constructs of other times and the tentativeness of current theories" (p. 403).

Of course, history cannot be mined indiscriminately. Historian Harold James (2012) at Princeton University cautions on just what we retain from the past. He remarked, "History can be a randomly mined source of fairy tales" (p. 87). The need to ensure that our history is not a mere fairy tale if it is to be of any use was recognized by the ancient Greek historian Polybius (circa 200–118 BCE). In attempting to explain to fellow Greeks how the Romans came to dominate the Ancient World, he noted in the introduction to *The Rise of the Roman Empire* (1980): "If history is deprived of the truth, we are left with nothing but an idle, unprofitable tale" (p. 43). For Polybius, knowledge of the past is our best guide to conduct.

If history was frequently mentioned as being insufficiently taught in finance programs, learning from current affairs was also singled out by sources as an often neglected area. Jim Liew, assistant professor in finance at the Johns Hopkins Carey Business School, remarked that the school is actually training students to review what goes on in the news and how quickly it affects markets. According to Professor Liew, such training is now a part of courses on advanced hedge funds and wealth management. He commented,

> For example, whenever there is an event which impacts markets, I challenge students to explain what happened and why. What was the magnitude and duration of the move? What is the market telling us? Students need to follow current events, to be hungry for knowledge, to be curious throughout their lives. They must constantly learn from the markets: As markets are ever changing, so too learning never ends.

In this connection, HSBC's King (2012) wrote,

> I lament that economists coming into the financial world struggle to relate what they have learned at university to economic developments in the real world. I have asked recent university leavers how much time they have spent in lectures and seminars on the financial crisis. Most admitted that the subject had not even been raised. This is profoundly disappointing. Not all students will be taught in a period of genuine economic upheaval—for good or for bad—but the chance to match their theoretical understanding with historic events reported all over the media is surely too good an opportunity to be dismissed so casually. (p. 24)

Behavioral Finance. Behavioral finance seeks to explain deviations from the rational behavior that is at the heart of mainstream finance theory. It does so by borrowing from the fields of individual and social psychology to explain deviations from rational behavior, such as biases, heuristics (rules of thumb), and problem framing. Actually, the term "behavioral finance" covers quite a wide range of approaches.

Although behavioral finance began to move into finance programs even before the 2002 Nobel Prize in Economics was awarded to the behavioral psychologist and economist Daniel Kahneman, many sources commented on the need to include more on behavioral finance in the curriculum for future investment professionals.[25] Professor Chang, for example, believes that the role of behavioral finance should be "strenuously revisited." The problems are (1) how to teach behavioral finance and (2) what to expect to be able to do with it.

The objective of behavioral finance is to improve our understanding of markets and our forecasts. It seeks to explain market movements as the result, at least in part, of the cognitive biases of market participants. In doing so, it attempts to understand how investors' judgments deviate from "rational" judgment. But although we can understand deviations from rational judgment in controlled experiments, how can we know what a "rational" judgment should be in financial markets? In a controlled experiment, we can know the "correct" answer, but in the case of financial markets, we do not know the correct answer. Hence, we are extrapolating from a simple situation, where the correct answer is known (in principle), to a complex situation, where the correct answer is not known.

In addition, many decisions in asset management are now performed with the use of computers and software procedures that are *not* subject to psychological, cognitive biases—although the programmers themselves may be. Exchange-traded funds—now valued at about 30% of overall equity volume—are a case in point:[26] Some ETFs are simply automated active strategies.

Sources had mixed opinions as to how market participants can use behavioral finance in making their investment decisions and, as a result, the place of behavioral finance in finance curricula.

Professor Kirman (2012) expressed the belief that it would be beneficial to teach both experimental economics and behavioral economics. The first, he argues, is a useful antidote to the standard assumptions of rationality because it examines how people actually make decisions in situations with uncertainty. As for behavioral finance, he argued that it reinforces experimental economics by revealing how important psychological considerations are in determining people's choices and behavior.

---

[25]The 2002 Nobel Prize in Economics was given to Daniel Kahneman "for having integrated insights from psychological research into economic science, especially concerning human judgment and decision making under uncertainty." A second prize that year went to Vernon Smith.

[26]Source: www.etftrends.com/2013/06/etf-trading-spikes-above-30-of-overall-volume/.

Some of the skepticism is related to how one can apply behavioral finance to investment decision making. Dr. Napier commented,

> Behavioral finance has two aspects. The first—that there are systematic predictable biases in markets—has not yet been that helpful. I do not know anyone who has been able to make money on this on a sustainable basis. The second—what we teach in our course on the history of financial markets at the Edinburgh Business School—is the need to understand one's own biases, to reduce the possibility of an error in judgment. We teach students practical things like to look at basic patterns, understand how to make better probability evaluations in order to reduce one's errors.

In a similar vein, Jarrod Wilcox, president of Wilcox Investment, commented, "In the area of behavioral finance, individual psychology is more relevant to dealing with clients and oneself as an investor." He believes that social psychology and fashion (herding) are more relevant for understanding markets.

As for looking at basic patterns, Dr. Napier suggested that we look at the financial markets more as a biological concept. He gave as an example a bird flying in the garden and said, "You cannot predict where a bird will land, but if you have observed it previously and know what it is likely to eat, you will be more accurate at forecasting where it will land."

As to the difficulty in actually using behavioral finance in investment management, PGGM's Jaap van Dam remarked, "Behavioral finance is an important addition, but it is often difficult to draw useful conclusions from the theory, for example, when managing money." Dr. Napier shares this perception.

Professor Lleo added,

> In my experience, behavioral finance is best presented as an evolution of financial decision theory rather than as a separate—or worse, competing—model. [Amos] Tversky and Kahneman (1974) started to work together on questions related to mathematical psychology—basically how good human beings are at computing the odds of events and making decisions accordingly. Their research naturally led them to finance. But we should not forget that their starting point was *decision theory* and that their most highly regarded contributions are positive: They add something to the existing body of knowledge rather than knocking down the building.

Statistics, Mathematics, and Modeling: More or Less of It? While the need to include more macroeconomics and the history of financial markets and the economy in the curriculum for future investment professionals was nearly universally shared, the need to teach statistics, mathematics, and modeling was also strongly felt by most sources, though sources also mentioned the need to develop, in parallel, the ability to critically evaluate model results. In finance, most models with real-world practicality are "learned" from past data and are subject to uncertainty. Most models are also sensitive to regime shifts, so their forecasting ability decays if markets undergo regime shifts.

Steven Greiner, FactSet's director of portfolio risk, remarked,

> The ability to determine patterns in data and separate signal from noise is *the* most important attribute to work in finance these days, and I am not referring to high-frequency trading, but there, it definitely is. Even fundamental managers these days squeeze their data through models and screening and are trying to learn how to read the data using analytics.

The question of teaching statistics, mathematics, and modeling to future investment professionals has two sides to it: Some curricula put too much emphasis on statistics, mathematics, and modeling, so students risk losing the big macroeconomic picture. Other curricula do not teach students enough statistics, mathematics, and modeling, so students receive insufficient training. They are unable to work with large datasets, apply the appropriate modeling techniques, and interpret the results. Learning how to collect and evaluate data and model, if only with simple modeling methods, should be part of every finance student's formal education.

Data are a main concern if our modeling is to be anchored in reality. But many schools do not make accessible to students the data feeds needed for financial modeling. One reason is the high cost of data feeds. With appropriate software programs, however, data feeds from, for example, Yahoo can be made accessible at no cost. Perhaps a greater problem is the availability of good historical data. In fact, creating a historical database is a complicated process because of the many corporate actions that affect firms, changes of tickers, and the need to associate price data with other data—such as, for example, inclusion of a stock in the S&P 500 or its exclusion. Creating a viable historical database is a project that exceeds the resources of most students.

Commenting on the need for students to be able to handle and model data, Professor Lleo remarked,

> Statistics and quantitative methods are increasingly relevant as more market and economic data are available than ever before and as computing power is getting ever cheaper. Even Excel can perform matrix multiplications and nonlinear optimizations (via Solver); it has a decent random-number generator and a large number of statistical functions. I firmly believe that financial analysts need a deeper understanding of statistics, probabilities, and statistical model building. A good knowledge of statistics and probability is also required if we want to move the standard curriculum beyond the sole normal distribution and cogently discuss many of the interesting advances achieved over the past 30 years.

The need to teach students to be proficient in statistics and modeling is not simply a question of learning the techniques, important as that is. The challenge is for students to go beyond the techniques to develop an intuitive approach to the application of the techniques. Paul Seabright (2012), professor of economics at the University of Toulouse (France), was referring to the education of economists when he wrote the following, but it is relevant also to students of finance:

> The teaching of statistics needs to be embedded in an understanding of empirical enquiry: what it is to do detective work on statistical data. This is hard to teach and must be done by example, and not just by precept—through collecting real data and trying to understand what the data show and not just by reading a textbook. Sometimes it is as important to understand what should not be concluded from data as what can be—not every published paper reporting a *t*-statistic of two or more has in fact established what it claims in its abstract, for instance. (p. 84)

An important aspect of the teaching of statistics is how to integrate human judgment with the results of data analysis. Broadly, this aspect is the domain of Bayesian statistics,[27] although alternative techniques are available. Dr. Wilcox mentioned the need for students to be introduced to Bayesian statistics, especially, he said, "as a framework for mixing qualitative and rigorous evidence-based conclusions." Bayesian statistics can update intuitive judgment of probability with the results of data analysis in the same logical framework of probability. Given the small size of samples available in finance and the impossibility of repeating observations with new data, an element of judgment is always present.

Some sources noted the need for students to become fast at processing data and to do so frequently in order to develop intuition. Professor Liew said that he throws a lot of data at students so that they can become proficient in processing and distilling data. The objective, he noted, is for students to build intuition out of the process.

Statistical inference is one aspect of mathematical modeling. The area that makes use of the most complicated mathematics is the pricing of derivatives. One of the authors of this book, Frank Fabozzi, is critical of the teaching of derivatives in a finance curriculum. He believes that, although for students to understand the factors and the underlying principle in the valuation of derivatives is important, allocating too much class time to this aspect of derivatives encourages students to conclude that valuing derivative assets is the critical aspect of the course. They are further encouraged in this belief because valuation is difficult and looks impressive from a mathematical perspective. Any professor who has worked in the investment management area knows, however, that derivatives pricing is rarely performed by a portfolio manager. When a complex derivative for a significant economic position must

---

[27]Bayesian statistics is a statistical theory in which statistical assumptions are themselves considered uncertain. In Bayesian statistics, prior probabilistic assumptions are modified in function of empirical evidence, producing a final probability assessment.

be priced, a quantitative group that is part of the asset management firm (the "modeling group" or "quant group") typically tackles the pricing.

Only after derivatives pricing is covered in the investment management course does the course turn to simple derivatives strategies. The key role of derivatives as means to control risk is not emphasized. Consequently, students joining the profession see derivatives as an exotic area because of its reliance on mathematics for derivatives pricing and fail to understand the key role of derivatives as a transactionally efficient vehicle for controlling risk.

Part of the problem when students transition from school to work is that students rarely understand that institutional portfolios are usually constructed by a team that includes a senior portfolio manager and a group of industry or sector analysts. A portfolio is constructed on the basis of all of the inputs of the team members. When adjusting a portfolio's risk, Fabozzi emphasizes, derivatives allow for the adjustment to be done efficiently without having to rebalance the cash positions that were included in the portfolio on the basis of the input from the portfolio team.

Risk Management. Risk management is at the heart of investment management, but many sources commented that it was not sufficiently taught in most finance programs. FactSet's Dr. Greiner remarked, "There is not nearly enough education in risk management for those who want to enter asset management as a profession. It is a big subject—a broad set of concepts and methods—and it is in few curricula." The situation is perhaps beginning to change. Professor Liew noted that since the 2007–09 financial crisis, the basics of risk management are now in most curricula.

Risk management enters asset management at the source because portfolio management is based on a notion of optimizing the risk–reward trade-off. But risk management is more than risk–return optimization. First, the notion of portfolio risk should be based on nonnormal distributions—a critical innovation in risk management. In fact, replacing normal distributions with fat-tailed distributions is only now becoming a key tenet of modern risk management, despite the fact that it was proposed more than 50 years ago by Benoit Mandelbrot (1963).

As Professor Fabozzi observed, managing the risk of large portfolios without changing much of the fundamental structure of portfolios—the result of the complex work of portfolio construction by the management team—generally requires the use of derivatives. The risk inherent in using derivatives has to be addressed separately.

We noted in Chapter 2 that credit risk deserves more attention, especially in view of the fact that two of the recent financial crises—Long-Term Capital Management and the subprime mortgage crisis—had credit risk at their sources. Another important source of risk that deserves more attention in curricula comes from accounting. For academia, accounting does not have the glamour of mathematical finance and is perceived to be a straightforward subject. But perhaps this reflects the lack of contact with the real world in many finance programs. This might change because investment managers now have the techniques to pick apart, for example, the notes in balance sheets. They can use data-mining techniques and advanced mathematical methods and, eventually, will be applying clustering techniques to find similarities among companies. Professor Logue remarked,

> Academics underestimate the significance of accounting, which consists of rules. One needs to read the footnotes, the 10-Ks and 10-Qs, while academia pooh-poohs accounting, given that it holds that markets are efficient. [Consider] how Citibank and its structuring of securities for Enron were sold to Vanguard and others as investment-grade securities while the bank knew that the information shown by Enron to Moody's and S&P was wrong. Citi had another set of information. Rating agencies believed Enron debt was $17 billion; Citi thought that it was $21 billion. In the end, Enron's debt was $27 billion to $28 billion.

By the end of November 2001, Enron's shares had plummeted to less than $1, after having experienced a high of $90.75 in mid-2000. In what was the biggest audit failure to that date, Enron shareholders lost an estimated $74 billion in the four years before the company's bankruptcy. Almost half of that amount was attributed to accounting fraud.

Another risk that must be understood is that models can break down when financial regimes change. The "meta-risk" of model failure has become an important part of risk management. Models in economics describe not laws of nature but a human artifact that is subject to change. Changes may invalidate models. For example, the policy of "quantitative easing" adopted by many central banks is widely considered to be behind today's rising stock markets. Models adapted to a situation of loose monetary policy may break down when tighter policies are adopted.

Systemic risk has been given little consideration to date in risk management curricula. As we noted in Chapter 2, however, in view of the most recent financial crisis, systemic risk has moved up on the research agenda. Attempts to model the boom–bust cycle of economies and financial markets make use of nonlinear dynamics and complex system theory. Network theory is being used to model aggregation and contagion phenomena that may explain crashes. Haldane (2012) and Kirman (2012), among others, argue that with the growing connectivity of economies and markets, aspiring risk managers would do well to study network theory to capture the system dynamics at work in a connected world. These techniques—network theory, (complex) system theory, and nonlinear dynamics, which have been proposed to model and understand systemic risk—are beyond the reach of most students in MBA programs who will seek a career in asset management. Indeed, most fund managers are still comfortable with the much criticized VaR to measure market risk. The advanced techniques are, however, appropriate for PhD students who will seek jobs in research departments and risk management.

Some argue, moreover, that risk management goes well beyond the classic idea of a quant seeing correlations in tails, to encompass, for example, operational risks (such as fraud and cyber-attacks) and even political risk.

How all of these risks can be packed into a curriculum is a challenge.

Ethics/Incentive Structures. Bruce Jacobs, principal of Jacobs Levy Equity Management, remarked on the importance of ethics when he said, "High ethical standards in all areas and at all levels are vital to the long-run survival of our industry." Yet, sources commented that such areas as business ethics disappeared from curricula in the 1990s.

Teaching ethics is clearly important. It is essential that students begin to learn how to work and prosper by keeping high ethical values. One human resources manager that we talked to for this study said that they place great importance on ethics: A strong sense of what can and cannot be done was one of several criteria cited for getting hired by the firm. High ethical standards are essential to maintaining trust and the regular functioning of markets. Fraud and unethical behavior have disruptive effects on markets; they have been cited as one reason small investors have withdrawn from financial markets.

Fabozzi, Focardi, and Jonas (2010) identified the need to regain investors' confidence as the biggest challenge to the investment management industry following the recent market crash. Regaining investors' confidence requires that investors believe that their interests are put before those of the investment management firm's owners and employees.

Some sources in academia said that they were working hard to integrate ethics into their courses. Professor Liew said that he tells his students, "If you keep 100% integrity at all times, you will have many opportunities in the future. Lose your integrity once, and you will not have those future opportunities as the trust has been forever broken."

The problem of ethics cannot be seen independently of the incentive systems put in place at asset management firms. HSBC's Dr. King (2012) noted that economists gain a much better understanding of why financial markets can fail by gaining a better understanding of how incentive structures can lead to undesirable outcomes.

Beyond ethics and incentive systems, however, lies the loftier issue of finance's role for good in society. In his address to the finance graduates of Yale University, Professor Shiller (2012b) made reference to the need for finance to reclaim its status as a force for good in society and to regain the trust of the public after having apparently contributed to thrusting the world economy into its worst crisis since the Great Depression. He told students,

> Finance, at its best, does not merely manage risk, but also acts as the steward of society's assets and an advocate of its deepest goals. Beyond compensation, the next generation of finance professionals will be paid its truest rewards in the satisfaction that comes with the gains made in democratizing finance—extending its benefits into corners of society where they are most needed. This is a new challenge for a new generation, and will require all of the imagination and skill that you can bring to bear. (p. 2)

In his book *Finance and the Good Society* (2012a), Professor Shiller argued that finance can be a powerful tool for solving our problems and increasing the general well-being.

Exhibit 4.1 summarizes subjects that academics and industry participants alike believe need to be (re)introduced to or reinforced in curricula that prepare students for future jobs in investment management.

Exhibit 4.1. Summary of Subjects that Should Be (Re)Introduced to or Reinforced in Finance Curricula

(Re)introduce/Reinforce	Reason
Macroeconomics	The economy drives markets; there is the need to develop macroeconomic reasoning behind the models.
History of macroeconomics	It would broaden thinking, give alternative ways for understanding macroeconomics.
History of financial markets	Future investment managers (and other practitioners) can learn from past events; the subject gives a range of the possible; it promotes understanding of financial phenomena.
Behavioral finance	It helps explain deviations from rational behavior and improves forecasts.
Statistics, math, and modeling	More data, more computing power, and the increasing complexity of financial markets require greater skill in working with data/models and understanding quantitative phenomena.
Risk management	Future investment managers (and other practitioners) will need to handle phenomena such as systemic risk that can destroy value.
Ethics, incentive structures	The profession needs to restore investor confidence.

5. How Will Future Professionals Land a Job in Investment Management?

Jobs in investment management are much sought after and hard to come by. Many candidates pursue the relatively few openings, so employers can be choosy. In addition, at least in the United States, the number of people directly employed in asset management firms at year-end 2012 (159,000) was still below the peak employed at year-end 2007 (168,000), according to the Investment Company Institute's most recent fact book (2013). We asked human resources managers at asset management firms what they look for in terms of profiles when hiring recent graduates. We also asked them whether there is a best path to landing a job in their firms.

Is There an Ideal Candidate for a Job in Investment Management?

The easy answer to this question is "no." The ideal candidate depends on the firm that is hiring and the position being filled, and it is time dependent.

Wanted: Analytical Ability. Nevertheless, from the previous chapters, we can see a rise in importance of solid economic reasoning and ability to see the big picture, including understanding the global macroeconomy and the (geo)political world. This same approach comes across in asset management firms' hiring. For example, HSBC's group chief economist and global head of economics and asset allocation research, Stephen King (2012), remarked as follows with reference to economists coming into the financial world, typically in research positions:

> Although many financial economists specialize in one particular country or region, increasingly they are expected to analyze the impact of events in one part of the world on other regions. Higher oil prices, slowing Chinese growth, new "south–south trade" and financial linkages—all have potentially large global effects. Our clients expect us to come up with analysis to cast light on these issues. . . . Despite our regional specialization, we cannot afford to treat each country as an island. (p. 22)

At some funds, the growing importance of good macroeconomic reasoning is leading to a change in hiring patterns. Jaap van Dam, head of strategy and research at the Dutch pension fund PGGM, observed,

> In the past 10 years, we hired a lot of engineers and econometricians. Going forward, we will look for people with a more fundamental understanding of the economy and markets. As a strategist, one is always fascinated by those that cite three digits behind the decimal point. They might be experts in one area but now we need people who can think "the big picture" whatever one's specialty is.

But we are having difficulty finding such people now. We are looking for people strong in economics but applied to understanding investment opportunities.

These views are shared by quantitative fund managers. Thomas Kieselstein, CIO and managing partner at Quoniam, whose formal education was in industrial engineering, commented,

> We will be looking more for people able to abstract from a technical view on a problem or a situation and able to at least make a judgment on the big picture. However, we find it very difficult to find talents that have these capabilities while also being exact and rigorous in their analysis.

Although quants are certainly not out of favor at asset management firms (the exception being traditional managers that typically do not hire quants anyway), most firms we talked to now want *both* math skills and economic reasoning skills in the same person. This change is important and has an impact on how universities and business schools prepare students (including PhDs) for jobs in investment management. It calls for a well-rounded curriculum that encompasses a broad spectrum of fundamental knowledge and quantitative skills.

Many sources said that the graduates they hire with master's degrees in finance or economics go on to fill positions on asset management teams or in sales and marketing whereas graduates with advanced degrees in engineering, mathematics, or physics are typically hired for multiasset or systemic groups or for roles in trading and risk management, where the ability to work with data and models is of great importance. But even on these teams, solid economic reasoning is increasingly being called for. Steven Greiner, director of portfolio risk at FactSet Research Systems, remarked,

> Physicists are usually very good hires for jobs that involve working with models and understanding their limitations because that is what 90% of them do—build models. They are trained not just to build a model but to think in terms of estimation error and confidence intervals. Additionally, modern physics is filled with nonlinear chaotic phenomena. So, unlike what most fundamentalists believe, they are already primed for dealing with financial data. Fundamentalists and old-school types think a physicist still deals with Newtonian determinism and that is why they believe scientifically trained people are improperly trained for the markets. They are dead wrong. The typical MBA view of physics comes from the last course they had in high school, where Newtonian classical mechanics (i.e., levers and pulleys) is what they learned. Quantum mechanics, fluid mechanics, and heat transfer are all about nonstationary phenomena, exactly like financial time series!

Still, firms that are hiring engineers, mathematicians, and physicists like to see that the student has taken some courses in economics or finance along the way. The firms want to hire people who have demonstrated an interest in the field of finance and who can think outside their own specialties.

Firms with a more traditional style of management may be hiring people with very different academic backgrounds. The head of human resources at one traditional asset manager said that the firm has always been open-minded about its new hires' fields of study. "We look for diversity," he commented. "We hire graduates with degrees in history, philosophy, the arts. They bring in different skills, have a different way of looking at things." This comment reflects the need for out-of-the-box thinking and creativity that many sources found lacking in graduates coming from traditional business schools teaching (often dogmatically) mainstream economic and finance theory.

Wanted: Broad Knowledge. When asked what asset management firms were looking for in graduate recruits, human resource managers most often replied: broad knowledge, analytical skills, sound (macroeconomic) reasoning, creativity, and out-of-the-box thinking. That many academic programs put too much emphasis on models was bemoaned by our sources. Michael Oliver, senior lecturer in finance at Open University and cofounder and director of the firm Global Partnership Family Offices, believes that many mathematical finance programs are divorced from events in the real world, which produces economists who can give you an equation for everything but who lack any broader knowledge.

The most recent financial crisis has created a demand for critical thinking. And broad knowledge opens the door to critical thinking. Someone who has developed interests not only in finance but also in questions of history, political economics, philosophy, science, and even the arts has more tools for critically analyzing theories and events. As Harvard University professor of political economy Benjamin Friedman (2012) noted, the financial crisis of 2007–2009 calls for a reexamination of the "dominant thinking." He wrote that in light of the crisis, "mainstream theories look not so much wrong as wrong-headed" (p. 123). HSBC's Dr. King (2012) believes that economists in financial markets who can provide only mathematical rigor are unlikely to be successful:

> Clients are well aware that even the best econometric models have a nasty habit of going wrong. An ability to talk about risks in a "big picture" framework is just as important, and mathematical rigour does not always lend itself to this imaginative approach. That need for breadth, in turn, means that the successful financial market economist should have a range of other skills and areas of knowledge. (p. 22)

The need for broad knowledge was also emphasized by Yale University professor of economics Robert Shiller (2012b). In delivering the 2012 graduation speech to the finance graduates at Yale University, he told graduates,

> Your training in financial theory, economics, mathematics, and statistics will serve you well. But, your lessons in history, philosophy, and literature will be just as important, because it is vital . . . that you have the right tools. . . .

93

Jim Liew, assistant professor of finance at Johns Hopkins Carey Business School, remarked, "I am of the school of thought that believes that anyone walking in a museum, reading a book on history, or whatever in function of one's interests can gain inspiration, produce innovative ideas through such seemingly orthogonal experiences." He added, "We do not really know how the brain functions. It works in many fascinating ways."

Wanted: The Ability to Communicate. The ability to communicate and to convince is important for just about any position at an asset management firm. With investors, the ability to communicate, to convincingly explain bad performance (whether because of model breakdown or whatever reason), is an important part of an asset manager's job. Sources at asset management firms have said that keeping communication lines open with investors during the recent market crash and explaining the losses helped retain assets under management (Fabozzi, Focardi, and Jonas 2010).

The ability to communicate with colleagues inside the firm is also important. Sources remarked on the need to communicate with one's peers, to question one's peers, to have conviction (but also to be able to change one's mind when presented with new facts or a stronger argument). Without strong communication skills, critical thinking may create conflicts and result in the rejection of good but poorly communicated ideas. Broad knowledge helps in finding convincing parallels, in objectivizing positions and ideas, and in placing them in a historical or scientific perspective.

Wanted: The Ability to Reason. Another important quality short-listed by human resources managers is the ability to reason, to take in large quantities of information, to separate the true information from the noise, and to analyze the data. Again, good macroeconomic reasoning requires an ability to see the big picture.

Sources remarked on candidates' needs to have a toolkit for how to analyze a problem that includes both analytical and mathematical skills. Candidates who pass all the initial hurdles are typically grilled by the hiring firm's asset managers. The objective is to test the candidate's reasoning and judgment. A source at a fundamental manager explained,

> The hiring process is based on a series of conversations. We make candidates talk about what they have done, why they made the decisions they made. We need to see through the person's thinking process. We also make them talk on topics such as current affairs for up to one hour. We want to see how they form their thoughts, test their assumptions, and how they conciliate competing ideas.

Wanted: Out-of-the-Box Thinking. Industry sources and academics cited the need for out-of-the-box thinking. Mr. Kieselstein summed up the general feeling when he commented, "There is too much emphasis on models and learning, too little on out-of-the-box thinking." Out-of-the-box thinking requires the ability to understand, to critique, and to find new angles from which to approach the problem at hand.

Key to teaching out-of-the-box thinking is to expose students to different ideas and points of view and explain the rationale behind each point of view. Exposure to different points of view gives students the mental flexibility required to think outside of established schemas. In a *Business Insider* interview with Sam Ro (2012), PIMCO's former CEO and co-CIO Mohamed El-Erian commented that he had been fortunate to have been influenced by ideas that value and promote diversity of thought and perspectives. Most significantly, he added,

> This included the importance of questioning, of pursuing cross-disciplinary work, of appreciating different cultural approaches, and of engaging in detailed scenario building that focuses both on baseline forecasts and also two-sided tail events. (p. 3)

Dogmatism is the enemy of innovation. It implies that only one point of view is acceptable; other points of view are rejected. We discussed in Chapter 1 what such dogmatism meant for crop yields in Stalin's Soviet Union.

Professor Liew emphasized the importance for students to learn to innovate, to think for themselves rather than follow the herd. "Don't dump assets just because everyone is dumping them," he said. The phenomenon of herding is a frequent behavioral pattern in financial markets: People pick up on a strategy that seems to work or a "hot" sector and everyone piles into it, but as Professor Liew observed, "It will not work forever." The dot-com bubble is often cited as an example of herding. Between the market high of March 2000 and the low of October 2002, investors lost $5 trillion as the valuation of dot-com stocks dived.

Wanted: High Interest in Financial Markets. It is also important that candidates be strongly motivated to work in the industry. The head of human resources at a large continental firm remarked, "In principle, we target and hire people with a drive, a fire for the industry." Another commented that the recruit having an interest in, a passion for, financial markets and what drives (global) markets is hugely important. How do firms test the strength of the motivation? One firm's staff answered,

> We ask questions in the on-line application process such as: Does the candidate invest personally as a hobby (assuming he or she has the money to do so). Is he or she part of an investment club? Has he or she taken a course in economics/finance together with their major?

Wanted: Humility. Another quality human resources managers said they are looking for is humility. The ideal candidate has a good idea of what can and what cannot be done and can admit that he or she might have made a mistake or might need to revise an opinion. One human resources manager said that the firm looks for persons with confidence but not arrogance and with some humility. Another noted that an arrogant person would not be hired. He or she "would not be useful," this source said.

Reminiscing about his days in school, Alan Brown, senior adviser at Schroders Investment Management, commented on the need for humility. Referring to the need to be critically aware of the limits of one's models and model results, he recalled,

> One of the most brilliant things I did when taking my degree was to have pitched camp in the rare books section in the [Cambridge] university library. There I came upon Newton's *Principia Mathematica* with Newton's comments in the margins. Newton was smart enough and humble enough to recognize that if an object is too big or too small or is moving too fast, it might not hold to his laws. Having just explained the movement of billiard balls and planets with one equation, that was pure genius.

Summary. **Exhibit 5.1** summarizes what industry sources said they look for in graduate recruits.

Exhibit 5.1.   Asset Management Firms' Recruiting

What Firms Are Seeking	Reason
Solid economic reasoning, the ability to see the big picture	Investment professionals must be able to analyze and explain the impact on their portfolio of events around the globe—political, environmental, and so on—and if called for, rebalance the portfolio.
The ability to combine rigorous mathematical analysis with sound economic thinking	Because our theories are weak and our models can break down, investment professionals need to abstract from a rigorous mathematical analysis and exercise judgment based on a fundamental understanding of the economy and markets.
Broad knowledge beyond the world of finance (e.g., history, political economics, philosophy, science, the arts)	Broad knowledge (1) provides more tools to critically analyze theories and events and evaluate model results and (2) enhances the ability to think creatively, to innovate.
The ability to reason	Investment professionals are inundated with large quantities of information/data; they must be able to take it in, separate the true information from the noise, analyze the information, exercise judgment, and formulate a sound investment decision.
Out-of-the-box thinking	An exposure to different ideas and different points of view and the ability to understand the rationale behind each point of view facilitate innovation as opposed to following the herd.
Humility	This quality includes the ability to admit that one might have made a mistake or need to revise a decision or opinion in view of new information.

Is There a Best School?

We asked human resources managers if any particular school would be best for someone who wants a job at their firm. Perhaps surprisingly, the typical reply was: "No, it is not a question of the school but of the individual. We hire from any school." Nevertheless, business school graduates seem to be well placed in the United States, and in France, graduates with a specialty in finance from *les grandes écoles*.[28] In Germany and the United Kingdom, many schools and universities are considered to do a good job of preparing students for jobs in investment management.

Referring to finance programs at business schools and universities, the human resources manager at a fundamental manager in the United Kingdom said,

> Sometimes students with rich academic investment experience have preconceived ideas about investing, but our approach to investing is less scientific and more like an art. We are not a quant boutique, so we are more interested in seeing the development of judgment, less in the math. Our young hires have a lot of history, science, languages. We want a healthy mix, with people with curiosity, the ability to analyze, and an interest in geopolitics.

Another source in Europe, who said that the firm hires from top universities but not from any supposed "top three," explained that the firm carries out a return on investment analysis of recruits and the schools they come from. The firm's experience is that the MBA program is a highly controversial program. This source has experienced negative added value in MBA hires. That is, the cost of recruits from these programs is high, and the value they add is not sufficient to cover the cost. This source said that the head of equity research recently reported that some undergraduates are outperforming MBAs. In this firm's experience, MBAs tend to be more ideological, arrogant, and unlikely to change their minds when confronted with others' opinions or new information. This source found that MBAs have, together with a lack of humility, high expectations in terms of salary and rapid career advancement. She wondered whether MBA schools are misselling their programs.

Getting through the Screening Process

Suppose that the graduate has initiated the typical process in applying for a job with an asset management firm. He or she will typically have gone through a series of online tests to determine, among other matters, his or her

---

[28]*Les grandes écoles* are typically state schools reputed to be the top institutions for students in engineering, mathematics, and the hard sciences but where the humanities are also an important part of the curriculum. Among *les grandes écoles* is École Polytechnique, founded in 1794 and given military status by Napoleon in 1805. More recently, business schools, including EDHEC and HEC, have also been given the rank of *grandes écoles* of business and management.

problem-solving and reasoning ability and psychometric fit with the job. The firm will then look at the candidates, their curriculum vitae, courses taken, and their grades to see if they have the requisite qualities. If candidates pass these hurdles and preliminary interviews, they are placed in front of "heads of desks" for (usually rigorous) interviews to test their skills. "In the recruiting process, we involve business managers a lot to challenge candidates," one human resources manager explained. "Some business managers can be very tough. They are interested in understanding the economic thinking of candidates."

Professor Liew has some advice for students who want to get a job at an asset management firm. He said,

> One needs to be very strong on the fundamentals, such as valuation, statistics, asset management techniques, macro and micro fundamentals. Suppose you studied to be a quant: Can you execute? You need to improve execution abilities. You need to be educated on what is going on *now*. You must be able to pick up the *Wall Street Journal* and cast a critical eye on articles—to pick up a journalist's biases, to critique the comments of a CEO, a CFO, to clearly see the big picture and, at the same time, not miss any of the fine details.

Indeed, in a previous study for the CFA Institute Research Foundation by the authors (2008), sources mentioned the danger of fundamental managers failing to take a critical view of the managers of corporations that their firm is considering investing in. The problem, a source for that study said, is that analysts may "fall in love" with a stock or be swayed by the chief financial officer they talk to.

Most Important Takeaway from Formal Education

We asked professors of economics and finance what they thought was the most important lesson students should take away from their formal education. We provide their answers here in no particular order:

On markets,

- realize that the real world is more complicated than academic theories suggest;

- be aware of the assumptions behind models and the limitations of models;

- understand the concepts and implications of disequilibrium, market instability, and crises;

- recognize that recurrent and frequent financial crises are the new norm;

- be aware that financial theories and models are simply heuristics (rules of thumb); and

- develop a deep understanding of the relationship between risk and return.

In general,

- know your history—in particular, the history of economics, finance, and financial markets;

- read broadly to develop your curiosity;

- don't be shy to ask questions;

- don't be afraid of the math;

- be aware of your biases;

- understand the heuristics you use;

- be hungry for knowledge;

- be gullible enough to understand any investment strategy, then pick it apart—first "gullible" because you need to suppress skepticism long enough to understand new and unfamiliar ideas and consider the possibility that they might be right (only later is it appropriate to criticize them); and

- continue to learn.

As for the last point, human resources managers at asset management firms we talked to emphasized how important it is that recruits continue to learn on the job. According to these sources, continuing to educate oneself demonstrates a new hire's commitment to a career in asset management.

Professor Liew noted that schooling is only the start of the process of becoming an asset manager. He said, "My experience is that, even after one has the right fundamentals, there will be lots of formal knowledge to pick up, lots of dead ends until one has acquired years of experience."

One comment was made specifically about the learning necessary to earn a CFA designation and participate in the CFA Program's continued learning. The head of human resources at a large European firm said, "The CFA Program is very important. We like the fact that the program is hard, that people have to work hard to learn."

Opinion Contributors

Following is a list of people whose opinions (either from the interview process or from publicly available documents) are cited in the monograph.

Ang, Andrew, Professor of Business at Columbia Business School and Chair of the Finance and Economics Division

Barro, Robert, Professor of Economics at Harvard University

Becker, Gary, Professor of Economics and Sociology at the University of Chicago and a Professor at the Booth School of Business. Awarded the 1992 Nobel Prize in Economics

Beinhocker, Eric, Executive Director of the Institute for New Economic Thinking's INET@Oxford research program at the University of Oxford

Black, Fischer, Director of the Quantitative Strategies Group at Goldman Sachs until his death in 1995. Previously taught at MIT Sloan School of Management and University of Chicago Booth School of Business

Brachinger, Hans Wolfgang, Professor in the Department of Quantitative Economics, University of Fribourg, Switzerland

Brown, Alan, Senior Advisor at Schroders Investment Management

Chang, Charles, Associate Professor and Director of the Master of Finance Program, Shanghai Advanced Institute of Finance, Shanghai Jiao Tong University, and Managing Partner of PM Legacy Capital

Cochrane, John, Adjunct Scholar at the Cato Institute, Professor of Finance at the University of Chicago Booth School of Business, and a research associate at the National Bureau of Economic Research

Colander, David C., Professor of Economics at Middlebury College

Cootner, Paul, financial economist who taught at both MIT and Stanford

Dever, Michael, CEO and Director of Research for Brandywine Asset Management

El-Erian, Mohamed, Former CEO and co-CIO of PIMCO, the California-based asset manager

Fama, Eugene, Robert R. McCormick Distinguished Service Professor of Finance at the University of Chicago Booth School of Business and recipient of the 2013 Nobel Prize in Economics

Friedman, Benjamin M., Professor of Political Economy, Harvard University

Glaeser, Edward F., Professor of Economics at Harvard University

Goetzmann, William N., Professor of Finance and Management Studies and Director of the International Center for Finance at the Yale School of Management

Grantham, Jeremy, cofounder of and market strategist at GMO

Greiner, Steven, Director of Portfolio Risk at FactSet Research Systems

Guerrien, Bernard, Professor of Economics at the University of Paris-Sorbonne

Gun, Ozgur, Professor of Economics at the University of Reims (France)

Haldane, Andrew, Executive Director for Financial Stability of the Bank of England

Hansen, Lars Peter, Professor of Economics, University of Chicago, and a corecipient of the 2013 Nobel Prize in Economics

Helbing, Dirk, Chair of Sociology, in particular of Modeling and Simulation, ETH Zurich

Jacobs, Bruce, Principal and cofounder of Jacobs Levy Equity Management

James, Harold, Princeton University Professor of History and International Affairs and Professor of History at European University Institute, Florence

Johnson, Neil, Professor of Physics, University of Miami, and head of new interdisciplinary research group in complexity

Kay, John, a distinguished British economist, visiting professor at London School of Economics (LSE), and a regular editorial contributor to the *Financial Times*

Kieselstein, Thomas, CFA, CIO and Managing Partner of Frankfurt-based quantitative asset manager Quoniam with more than €18 billion in assets under management

King, Stephen, HSBC's Group Chief Economist and Global Head of Economics and Asset Allocation Research

Kirman, Alan, Professor Emeritus of Economics at the University of Aix-Marseille III and at the École des Hautes Études en Sciences Sociales

Lefeuvre, Evariste, CIO and Chief Economist for the Americas at Natixis Global Asset Management

Liew, Jim, Lecturer in Finance, Quantitative Finance, and Hedge Funds at the Johns Hopkins Carey Business School

Lleo, Sébastien, Professor of Finance at NEOMA Business School (formed by the recent merger of Rouen Business School and Reims Management School France) and visiting professor at the Frankfurt School of Finance and Management

Lo, Andrew, Professor of Finance at the MIT Sloan School of Management and Director of MIT's Laboratory for Financial Engineering. Together with Lars Peter Hansen, corecipient of the 2013 Nobel Prize in Economics, Lo codirects the Macro Financial Modeling group at the Becker Friedman Institute

Logue, Dennis E., Professor of Management, Emeritus at the Tuck School of Business, Dartmouth, and Chair of the Board of Directors at Ledyard Financial Group

Lucas, Robert, Professor of Economics, University of Chicago, and 1995 recipient of the Nobel Prize in Economics

Lux, Thomas, Professor of Economics, University of Kiel (Germany), and Head of Financial Markets and Macroeconomic Activity

May, Robert M., Professor at Oxford and Imperial College; former Chief Scientific Adviser to the UK government and Head of the UK Office of Science and Technology

McCauley, Joseph, Professor of Physics at the University of Houston

Merton, Robert C., Professor of Economics at the MIT Sloan School of Management and a corecipient of 1997 Nobel Prize in Economics

Montier, James, a member of GMO's Asset Allocation Team

Napier, Russell, Consultant with CLSA Asia-Pacific Markets and a director of the course "A Practical History of Financial Markets" at the Edinburgh Business School

Naumer, Hans-Joerg, Head of Global Capital Equity Markets and Thematic Research, Allianz Global Advisors

Nusseibeh, Saker, CEO and Head of Investment at Hermes Fund Managers

Oliver, Michael J., Senior Lecturer in Finance at the Open University and cofounder and Director of Global Partnership Family Offices

Olivier, Jacques, Professor of Finance and Program Director of the Master in Finance at HEC (Hautes Etudes de Commerce, France)

Ormerod, Paul, British economist conducting research in complexity, complex systems, nonlinear feedback, and boom-and-bust economic cycles

Pfleiderer, Paul, Professor of Finance at the Stanford Graduate School of Business and cofounder of portfolio management software firm Quantal International

Qian, Edward, CIO, Head of Multi-Asset Research at the quantitative asset management firm PanAgora

Romer, David, Professor of Political Economy at the University of California, Berkeley

Seabright, Paul, Professor of Economics in the Industrial Economics Institute and Toulouse School of Economics at the University of Toulouse (France)

Shiller, Robert J., Professor of Economics at Yale University and a corecipient of the 2013 Nobel Prize in Economics

Sornette, Didier, Professor of Entrepreneurial Risks at ETH Zurich, Professor of Finance at the Swiss Finance Institute, Director of the Financial Crisis Observatory and founding member of the Risk Center at ETH Zurich

Stiglitz, Joseph, Professor of Economics at Columbia University and 2001 corecipient of the Nobel Prize in Economics

Taleb, Nassim, Professor of Risk Engineering at Polytechnic Institute of New York University

Valtonen, Erik, CEO, Blue Diamond Asset Management AG, Zurich. Formerly head of Risk Management and CIO at Swedish buffer fund AP3

Van Dam, Jaap, Head of Strategy and Research, Dutch healthcare workers' pension fund PGGM

Waring, Barton, former CIO of Investment Policy and Strategy at Barclays Global Investors and now an author and lecturer on investment policy and strategy

Wilcox, Jarrod, President of Wilcox Investment; formerly Professor at MIT's Sloan School of Management

Woolley, Paul, cofounder of the UK fund manager GMO-Woolley and founder of the Paul Woolley Centre for the Study of Capital Markets Dysfunctionality at the London School of Economics

Not included: human resources managers at asset management firms who were promised anonymity.

References

Adler, David. 2012. *The New Field of Liquidity and Financial Frictions*. Charlottesville, VA: CFA Institute Research Foundation.

Ahamed, Liaquat. 2009. *Lords of Finance: The Bankers Who Broke the World*. New York: Penguin Press.

Ang, Andrew. Forthcoming. *Asset Management. A Systematic Approach to Factor Investing*. Oxford, UK: Oxford University Press.

Barro, Robert. 2009. "Lucas Roundtable: Don't Fault the Economists." *Economist* (8 August): http://www.economist.com/blogs/freeexchange/2009/08/lucas_roundtable_dont_fault_th.

Beinhocker, Eric D. 2007. *The Origin of Wealth: The Radical Remaking of Economics and What It Means for Business and Society*. Boston, MA: Harvard Business Review Press.

Black, Fischer. 1986. "Noise." *Journal of Finance*, vol. 41, no. 3 (July):529–543.

Black, Fischer, and Myron Scholes. 1973. "The Pricing of Options and Corporate Liabilities." *Journal of Political Economy*, vol. 81, no. 3 (May–June):637–654.

Brachinger, Hans Wolfgang. 2002. "Measurement of Risk." Switzerland: University of Fribourg.

Brown, Alan. 2013. "Dynamic Asset Allocation and Fund Governance." White paper, 300 Club (April): http://www.the300club.org/Portals/0/Dynamic_Asset_Allocation_and_Fund_Governance_FINAL_220413.pdf.

Cassidy, John. 2010. "An Interview with Eugene Fama." In the author's column "Rational Irrationality," *New Yorker* (13 January): http://www.newyorker.com/online/blogs/johncassidy/2010/01/interview-with-eugene-fama.html.

CFA Society of the UK. 2011. "CFA Society of the UK's Response to the Joint Committee on the Draft Financial Services Bill" (https://secure.cfauk.org/assets/2481/CFA_UK_response_Joint_Committee_call_for_evidence_FINAL.pdf).

Colander, David. 2007. *The Making of an Economist, Redux*. Princeton, NJ: Princeton University Press.

———. 2009. "What Makes a Good Economist?" In *What's the Use of Economics? Teaching the Dismal Science after the Crisis*. 2009 edition. Edited by Diane Coyle. London, UK: London Publishing Partnership.

Cootner, Paul H. 1964. *The Random Character of Stock Market Prices*. Cambridge, MA: MIT Press.

Dever, Michael, and John Uebler. 2012. "What 'Drives' Stock Market Performance?" Seeking Alpha (13 April): http://seekingalpha.com/article/496741-what-drives-stoc k-market-performance.

El-Erian, Mohamed. See Ro (2012).

Fabozzi, Frank J., Sergio M. Focardi, and Caroline Jonas. 2008. *Challenges in Quantitative Equity Management.* Charlottesville, VA: CFA Institute Research Foundation.

Fabozzi, Frank J., and Sergio M. Focardi. 2010. "Diversification: Should We Be Diversifying Trends?" *Journal of Portfolio Management,* vol. 36, no. 4 (Summer):1–4.

Fabozzi, Frank J., Sergio M. Focardi, and Caroline Jonas. 2010. *Investment Management after the Global Financial Crisis.* Charlottesville, VA: CFA Institute Research Foundation.

Fabozzi, Frank J., Sergio M. Focardi, and Petter N. Kolm. 2006. *Trends in Quantitative Finance.* Charlottesville, VA: CFA Institute Research Foundation.

Fama, Eugene F. 1963a. "Mandelbrot and the Stable Paretian Hypothesis." *Journal of Business,* vol. 36, no. 4 (October):420–429.

———. 1963b. The Distribution of Daily Differences of Stock Prices: A Test of Mandelbrot's Stable Paretian Hypothesis. Doctoral dissertation, Graduate School of Business, University of Chicago.

———. 1965. "The Behavior of Stock-Market Prices." *Journal of Business,* vol. 38, no. 1 (January):34–105.

———. 1970. "Efficient Capital Markets: A Review of Theory and Empirical Work." *Journal of Finance,* vol. 25, no. 2 (May):383–417.

Fama, Eugene F., and Kenneth R. French. 1992. "The Cross-Section of Expected Stock Returns." *Journal of Finance,* vol. 47, no. 2 (June):427–465.

———. 1993. "Common Risk Factors in the Returns on Stocks and Bonds." *Journal of Financial Economics,* vol. 33, no. 1 (February):3–56.

Focardi, Sergio M., and Frank J. Fabozzi. 2012. "What's Wrong with Today's Economics? The Current Crisis Calls for an Approach to Economics Rooted More on Data Than on Rationality." *Journal of Portfolio Management,* vol. 38, no. 3 (Spring):104–119.

Foley, Stephen. 2013. "Physicists and the Financial Markets." *FT Magazine* (18 October): http://www.ft.com/intl/cms/s/2/8461f5e6-35f5-11e3-952b-00144feab7de. html#axzz2i8AYZN6D.

Friedman, Benjamin M. 2010. "Reconstructing Economics in Light of the 2007–? Financial Crisis." *Journal of Economic Education,* vol. 41, no. 4:391–397.

————. 2012. "Rethinking Macroeconomics in the Wake of the Financial Crisis." In *What's the Use of Economics? Teaching the Dismal Science after the Crisis.* Edited by Diane Coyle. London, UK: London Publishing Partnership.

Galbraith, John Kenneth. 1987. *The History of Economics: The Past as the Present.* Edition of 1991 available from Penguin Books.

Galilei, Galileo. 1623. *The Assayer.* Available in various books; for example, chapter 7 in *The Essential Galileo.* Edited by Maurice A. Finocchiaro. Indianapolis, IA: Hackett Publishing.

Glaeser, Edward. 2012. "Experience Matters in the Education of Economists." In *What's the Use of Economics?: Teaching the Dismal Science after the Crisis.* Edited by Diane Coyle. London, UK: London Publishing Partnership.

Goetzmann, William N., Catherine Labio, K. Geert Rouwenhorst, Timothy G. Young, and Robert J. Shiller. 2013. *The Great Mirror of Folly: Finance, Culture, and the Crash of 1720.* Yale Series in Economic and Financial History. New Haven, CT: Yale University Press.

Guerrien, Bernard, and Ozgur Gun. 2011. "Efficient Market Hypothesis: What Are We Talking About?" *Real-World Economics Review,* no. 56 (11 March):19–30 (http://www.paecon.net/PAEReview/issue56/whole56.pdf).

Haldane, Andrew G. 2009. "Rethinking the Financial Network." Speech to the Financial Student Association, Amsterdam, Netherlands (28 April): http://www.bis.org/review/r090505e.pdf.

Haldane, Andrew. 2012. "Old Wine, New Bottles." In *What's the Use of Economics? Teaching the Dismal Science after the Crisis.* Edited by Diane Coyle. London, UK: London Publishing Partnership.

Haldane, Andrew G., and Robert M. May. 2011. "Systemic Risk in Banking Ecosystems." *Nature,* vol. 469 (20 January):351–355.

Investment Company Institute. 2013. *2013 Investment Company Fact Book:* http://www.ici.org/pdf/2013_factbook.pdf.

Jacobs, Bruce I. 1999. *Capital Ideas and Market Realities: Option Replication, Investor Behavior, and Stock Market Crashes.* Malden, MA: Blackwell.

————. 2004. "Risk Avoidance and Market Fragility." *Financial Analysts Journal,* vol. 60, no. 1 (January/February):26–30.

————. 2009. "Tumbling Tower of Babel: Subprime Securitization and the Credit Crisis." *Financial Analysts Journal,* vol. 65, no. 2 (March/April):17–30.

Jacobs, Bruce I., and Kenneth N. Levy. 2012. "Leverage Aversion and Portfolio Optimality." *Financial Analysts Journal,* vol. 68, no. 5 (September/October): 89–94.

————. 2013. "Leverage Aversion, Efficient Frontiers, and the Efficient Region." *Journal of Portfolio Management,* vol. 39, no. 3 (Spring):54–64.

————. 2014. "Traditional Optimization Is Not Optimal for Leverage-Averse Investors." *Journal of Portfolio Management*, vol. 40, no. 2 (Winter):30–40.

James, Harold. 2012. "Finance Is History!" In *What's the Use of Economics? Teaching the Dismal Science after the Crisis.* Edited by Diane Coyle. London, UK: London Publishing Partnership.

Jensen, Michael C. 1978. "Some Anomalous Evidence Regarding Market Efficiency." *Journal of Financial Economics*, vol. 6, no. 2–3:95–101.

Johnson, Neil. 2011. "Proposing Policy by Analogy Is Risky." *Nature*, vol. 469:302.

Kay, John. 2007. "The Fruitless Search for Exact Knowledge." *Financial Times* (16 October): http://www.ft.com/intl/cms/s/0/75a30c34-7bfc-11dc-be7e-0000779fd2ac. html#axzz2fdCMeSSu.

————. 2010. "The Political Constraints of the Eurozone and the Future of the EU." Presentation given at the Third Annual CFA Institute European Investment Conference, Copenhagen, Denmark (8–10 November).

————. 2012. "The Map Is Not the Territory: An Essay on the State of Economics." In *What's the Use of Economics? Teaching the Dismal Science after the Crisis.* Edited by Diane Coyle. London, UK: London Publishing Partnership.

Keynes, John Maynard. 1936. *The General Theory of Employment, Interest and Money.* Available in several forms; for example, online from CreateSpace Independent Publishing Platform (15 November 2011).

Kindleberger, Charles A., and Robert Z. Aliber. 1978. *Manias, Panics, and Crashes: A History of Financial Crises.* 5th ed. 2005. Hoboken, NJ: Wiley & Sons.

King, Stephen. 2012. "Economists in the Financial Markets." In *What's the Use of Economics? Teaching the Dismal Science after the Crisis.* Edited by Diane Coyle. London, UK: London Publishing Partnership.

Kirman, Alan. 1992. "Whom or What Does the Representative Individual Represent?" *Journal of Economic Perspectives*, vol. 6, no. 2 (Spring):117–136.

————. 2009. "Economic Theory and the Crisis," *Real-World Economics Review*, no. 51 (1 December 2009):80–83 (http://www.paecon.net/PAEReview/issue51/ Kirman51.pdf).

————. 2010. "The Economic Crisis Is a Crisis for Economic Theory." *CESifo Economic Studies*, vol. 56, no. 4:498–535.

————. 2012. "The Economy and Economic Theory in Crisis." In *What's the Use of Economics? Teaching the Dismal Science after the Crisis.* Edited by Diane Coyle. London, UK: London Publishing Partnership.

Knight, Frank H. 1921. *Risk, Uncertainty, and Profit.* Hart, Schaffner, and Marx Prize Essays, no. 31. New York: Houghton Mifflin (http://www.econlib.org/library/ Knight/knRUP.html).

Kolm, Petter K., Reha Tütüncu, and Frank J. Fabozzi. 2014. "60 Years of Portfolio Optimization: Practical Challenges and Current Trends." *European Journal of Operational Research*, vol. 234, no. 2 (April):356–371.

Kondratiev, Nikolai D. 1925. *The Major Economic Cycles.* The 2004 edition reproduced at this website was published in Moscow, Russia, by the International Kondratieff Foundation: http://www.library.newparadigm.ru/files/b22-2.pdf.

Kuhn, Thomas S. 1962. *The Structure of Scientific Revolutions.* 3rd ed. Chicago, IL: University of Chicago Press.

Laloux, L., P. Cizeau, J.-P. Bouchaud, and M. Potters. 2000. "Random Matrix Theory and Financial Correlations." *International Journal of Theoretical and Applied Finance*, vol. 3, no. 3 (July):391–397.

Ledoit, Olivier, and Michael Wolf. 2003. "Improved Estimation of the Covariance Matrix of Stock Returns with an Application to Portfolio Selection." *Journal of Empirical Finance*, vol. 10, no. 5 (December):603–621.

Lefeuvre, Evariste. 2012. "Modern Modelling and Return Prediction." *Natixis* (6 December).

Lo, Andrew. 2004. "The Adaptive Markets Hypothesis." *Journal of Portfolio Management*, 30th Anniversary Issue, vol. 30, no. 5:15–29.

Lo, Andrew W. 2012. "What Post-Crisis Changes Does the Economics Discipline Need?" In *What's the Use of Economics? Teaching the Dismal Science after the Crisis.* Edited by Diane Coyle. London, UK: London Publishing Partnership.

Longin, François, and Bruno Solnik. 1995. "Is the Correlation in International Equity Returns Constant: 1960–1900?" *Journal of International Money and Finance*, vol. 14, no. 1:3–26.

Lucas, Robert. 2009. "In Defence of the Dismal Science." *Economist* (6 August): http://www.economist.com/node/14165405.

Lux, Thomas. 2011. "Network Theory Is Sorely Required." *Nature*, vol. 469:303.

Mackay, Charles. 1841. *Extraordinary Popular Delusions and the Madness of Crowds.* 2003 edition published by Dover Publications, Mineola, New York.

Malkiel, Burton G. 1973. *A Random Walk Down Wall Street.* New York: W.W. Norton & Co.

———. 2011. "The Efficient Market Hypothesis and the Financial Crisis." In *Rethinking the Financial Crisis.* New York: Russell Sage.

Mandelbrot, Benoit. 1963. "The Variation of Certain Speculative Prices." *Journal of Business*, vol. 36, no. 4 (October):394–419.

Markowitz, Harry. 1952. "Portfolio Selection." *Journal of Finance*, vol. 7:77–91.

McCauley, Joseph. 2009. *Dynamics of Markets: The New Financial Economics.* 2nd ed. Cambridge, UK: Cambridge University Press.

Merton, Robert. 1973. "An Intertemporal Capital Asset Pricing Model." *Econometrica*, vol. 41, no. 5 (September):867–887.

Minsky, Hyman P. 1986. *Stabilizing an Unstable Economy*. New Haven, CT: Yale University Press (http://www.scribd.com/doc/11626149/Minsky-Stabilizing-an-Unstable-Economy-Complete).

———. 1992. "The Financial Instability Hypothesis." Working Paper No. 74, Jerome Levy Economics Institute of Bard College (May): http://www.levyinstitute.org/pubs/wp74.pdf.

Montier, James. 2012. "The Flaws of Finance." White Paper based on a speech delivered at the 65th CFA Institute Annual Conference in Chicago (6 May 2012).

Napier, Russell. 2005. *The Anatomy of the Bear: Lessons from Wall Street's 4 Great Bottoms*. 2nd ed. published in 2007; updated edition, in 2009. Petersfield, UK.: Harriman House.

Naumer, Hans-Joerg. 2013. "Focus: Crises: The Creative Power of Destruction." Allianz GI Global Capital Markets and Thematic Research, Allianz Global Investors (March).

Newton, Isaac. 1687. *Principia Mathematica*. Available in several forms; for example, as *The Principia: Mathematical Principles of Natural Philosophy*. Snowball Publishing, 2010.

Nocera, Joe. 2009. "Poking Holes in a Theory on Markets." *NY Times* (5 June): http://www.nytimes.com/2009/06/06/business/06nocera.html?pagewanted=all&_r=0.

Nusseibeh, Saker. 2012. "Political Risk: The Impact on Investors." Hermes Thought Piece (September).

Oliver, Michael J. 2008. "Are Economists Being Too Rigorous about the Wrong Things?" *Financial Times* (25 February): http://www.ft.com/cms/s/0/91255f9c-e345-11dc-803f-0000779fd2ac.html#axzz2u0FM4t6E.

Ormerod, Paul, and Dirk Helbing. 2012. "Back to the Drawing Board for Macroeconomics." In *What's the Use of Economics? Teaching the Dismal Science after the Crisis*. Edited by Diane Coyle. London, UK: London Publishing Partnership.

Pepper, Gordon, and Michael J. Oliver. 2006. *The Liquidity Theory of Asset Prices*. New York: Wiley Finance.

Pfleiderer, Paul. 2012. "Is Modern Portfolio Theory Dead? Come On." *TechCrunch* (11 August): http://techcrunch.com/2012/08/11/is-modern-portfolio-theory-dead-come-on/.

Planck, Max. 1949 or 1950. "Scientific Autobiography and Other Papers." *American Journal of Physics*, vol. 18, no. 2. These papers are available in a book of the same title published 1968 in New York by the Philosophical Library.

Plerou, V., P. Gopikrishnan, B. Rosenow, L.A.N. Amaral, and H.E. Stanley. 1999. "Universal and Nonuniversal Properties of Cross-Correlations in Financial Time Series." *Physical Review Letters*, vol. 83:1471–1474.

Polybius. 1980 edition. *The Rise of the Roman Empire*. London, UK: Penguin Classics.

Rachev, Svetlozar T., Christian Menn, and Frank J. Fabozzi. 2005. *Fat-Tailed and Skewed Asset Return Distributions: Implications for Risk Management, Portfolio Selection, and Option Pricing*. Hoboken, NJ: John Wiley & Sons.

Reinhart, Carmen M., and Kenneth S. Rogoff. 2009. *This Time Is Different: Eight Centuries of Financial Folly*. Princeton, NJ: Princeton University Press.

Ro, Sam. 2012. "El-Erian: These Are the Institutions and People Who Shaped the Way I Think." *Business Insider* (25 September): http://www.businessinsider.com/el-erian-people-who-shaped-the-way-i-think-2012-9?op=1#ixzz2MmdVsAJH.

Romer, David. 2013. "Preventing the Next Catastrophe: Where Do We Stand?" Presentation at the IMF conference "Rethinking Macro Policy II: First Steps and Early Lessons" (9 May): http://blog-imfdirect.imf.org/2013/05/03/preventing-the-next-catastrophe-where-do-we-stand/.

Seabright, Paul. 2012. "The Education of Economists in the Light of the Financial Crisis." In *What's the Use of Economics? Teaching the Dismal Science after the Crisis*. Edited by Diane Coyle. London, UK: London Publishing Partnership.

Sharpe, William F., and Lawrence G. Tint. 1990. "Liabilities: A New Approach." *Journal of Portfolio Management*, vol. 16, no. 2 (Winter):5–10.

Shiller, Robert J. 1981. "Do Stock Prices Move Too Much to Be Justified by Subsequent Changes in Dividends?" *American Economic Review*, vol. 71, no. 3 (June):421–436.

———. 2005. *Irrational Exuberance*. 2nd ed. Princeton, NJ: Princeton University Press.

———. 2010a. "How Should the Financial Crisis Change How We Teach Economics?" *Journal of Economic Education*, vol. 41, no. 4:403–409.

———. 2010b. "Using Behavioral Finance to Better Understand the Psychology of Investors." *Institutional Investor Magazine* (May): http://www.institutionalinvestor.com/Article/2485942/Asset-Management/Using-Behavioral-Finance-to-Better-Understand-the-Psychology-of-Investors.html#.UkHEdibD_Xk.

———. 2012a. *Finance and the Good Society*. Princeton, NJ: Princeton University Press.

———. 2012b. "My Speech to the Finance Graduates" (22 May): http://www.project-syndicate.org/commentary/my-speech-to-the-finance-graduates.

———. 2013. "Bubbles Forever." Project Syndicate (17 July): http://www.
project-syndicate.org/print/the-never-ending-struggle-with-speculative-bubbles-by
-robert-j--shiller.

Sonnenschein, Hugo. 1972. "Market Excess-Demand Functions." *Econometrica*, vol.
40, no. 3:549–563.

Sornette, Didier, and Peter Cauwels. 2012. "The Illusion of the Perpetual Money
Machine." Notenstein Academy White Paper Series (http://arxiv.org/ftp/arxiv/
papers/1212/1212.2833.pdf).

Stiglitz, Joseph. 2013. "The Lessons of the North Atlantic Crisis for Economic
Theory and Policy." (9 May): http://blog-imfdirect.imf.org/2013/05/03/the-lessons-o
f-the-north-atlantic-crisis-for-economic-theory-and-policy/.

Taleb, Nassim. 2010. *The Black Swan*. 2nd ed. New York: Random House Trade
Paperbacks.

Tversky, Amos, and Daniel Kahneman. 1974. "Judgment under Uncertainty:
Heuristics and Biases." *Science*, vol. 185, no. 4157 (27 September):1124–1131.

Woolley, Paul. 2010. "Why Are Financial Markets So Inefficient and Exploitative—
and a Suggested Remedy." In *The Future of Finance and the Theory That Underpins It*.
The LSE Report. London School of Economics and Political Science.

Ziemba, William T., and John M. Mulvey, eds. 1998. *Worldwide Asset and Liability
Modeling*. Cambridge, UK: Cambridge University Press.